AUTOBIOGRAPHY OF A MISFIT

AUTOBIOGRAPHY OF A MISFIT

Selected writings of Capt. Alan Richard Illeigh Hiley

HILEY

edited by Janet A. Hiley

Autobiography of a Misfit: Selected Writings of Capt. Alan Richard Illeigh Hiley.
Edited by Janet A. Hiley.
Copyright © 2022 Janet A. Hiley.
Preface, intro., endnotes, compiled by Janet A. Hiley.
All rights reserved.

Presence Pathway Press
presencepathway@gmail.com

No part of this book may be reproduced in any manner whatsoever without written permission except in the case of brief quotations embodied in critical articles and reviews.

Cover Design: J.A. Hiley
Front Cover:
Capt. A.R. Hiley on porch, family archive, J.A. Hiley
View from Glengarry Hilltop, J. A. Hiley
Back Cover:
Sholem Cabin, Glengarry Rd., J. A. Hiley
Portrait of Capt. Alan R. Hiley, *The Man in the Red Tie*, painted by E. Spencer Macky, Hiley archive

First Printing, 2022
ISBN 978-0-578-32260-5

*For my brother Brian
and the journey in love*

SHOLEM

*O sublime nature,
in thy stillness let my heart rest.*

~ Hazrat Inayat Khan

Contents

Dedication   v

Preface   1

Introduction   3

I
AUTOBIOGRAPHY OF A MISFIT

1. Foreword   6
2. Childhood Days in England   7
3. The Day the Admiralty Called   37
4. Later Boyhood   43
5. A Clipper Ship in 'Eighty   52
6. On Sir Clements Markham   72

II
STORIES & REFLECTIONS

7. Bicoachi (Mexico)   76
8. Dog-Gone Memories   80
9. Prospecting Before Gasoline Came   100
10. Helvetia   110

11	Range Lore	112
12	Sholem	123
13	Going Home	132
14	A Faith	134
15	Uncured Speech	139
16	The Ghost of a Love	152
17	The Story of Capt. Alan R. I. Hiley coming to Felton	154
18	Letter Excerpts & Notes	156
19	Reflection	160

Notes on the Family	163
Additional Photos	165
Other Publications	169
References	170
Acknowledgments	171
About the Author	172

Preface

When I left New Mexico and moved to California in 1984, I met my father's cousin, Alan Hiley, Jr., in Felton. At that time he was about to retire, along with his wife Betty, from their Redwood Shop to the hilltop which his father had purchased in 1906 and where he had been born. The original cabin had been preserved, complete with the original furnishings and books.

Alan Jr. shared with me a trunk filled with his father's writings and mementos, and we spent many hours over many years going through them and talking them over. His mother, Alma, had kept the stories and memories alive for her son, and so there was much family lore. After the death of Alan, Sr. in 1930, until 1970 Alma kept up a correspondence with her sister-in-law Frances in England. I was given those delightful letters.

It was Frances, the youngest child of Rev. Walter Hiley and Henrietta Jemima Forbes Hiley, who pieced together some family history, gleaning much from her mother's diaries for those of us in the "States." And for many years, that was all we had. Finding Alan's Autobiography was therefore a rich gift. In 2005, I traveled to England and met the wonderful Peter Hiley (son of Alan's brother Ernest), who filled in more. In 2011, I visited some of the family places mentioned in the Autobiography and Aunt Frances' papers, as well as Scotland. I was struck by how vividly accurate Alan's memories were of Hyde Hall and Brent Pelham.

As I prepared these manuscripts for publication, I was able to piece together more of Alan's life and influences. For all that he appeared rough around the edges, he was soft-spoken, and voraciously and broadly well-read— from literature and philosophy to spirituality and poetry, along with authentic tales of adventure. In addition to his adventures at sea, South Africa, and the frontier of the "Wild West," he passed through London, Paris, Italy, New York, Los Angeles, San Francisco, New Zealand, Brazil, and other places. He took an uncomfortably independent stand by siding with the Burghers against his home country in the Boer War, volunteering with an American scout brigade without pay. He continued to correspond with Sir Clements Markham, his heroes and comrades in the Boer War, and with artists, writers, actors, musicians, philosophers and poets whom he befriended. One of his artist friends, the San Francisco bookbinder Hazel Dreiss, bound some special editions for him, including a large empty volume in which he and Alma pasted their favorite poems. He wrote prolifically, with Alma typing and editing. He was well aware of his choices and all that they implied, whether by volition or circumstance. As a privileged young child in England's Victorian era (as an adult visiting, he was present for the Jubilee), he emerged as a male in a Colonial era; though he rebelled, he still carried the advantages of his upbringing. I have left his words unchanged, as they were written in the context of that era. No doubt he, too, would change further in the current era.

I have enjoyed getting to know Alan through his mementos, ledgers, collections, musings and manuscripts, and the family legends about him. I hope you, the reader, enjoy his stories, and imagining times not so long ago, yet far away, with characters somehow very familiar.

Janet A. Hiley
June 2022

Introduction

Memoirs of a philosophic adventurer

Born in the Victorian England of 1868, in a class and era of boarding schools and set pathways, as a boy Captain Alan R. I. Hiley was robust, athletic and adventurous. At an early age he stood out as both a leader and an independent spirit, not fitting into the strictures and conventions of the day. Thought a "misfit" in some traditional schools (perhaps he would have been more suited to today's varied educational approaches), at the young age of 10 he was enrolled in a ship/school aimed at training future naval officers. This five-year stint started him, prematurely and precipitously, on a course of nomadic adventures around the world, eventually in the West of North America. He settled finally in the Coastal Redwood Range of Santa Cruz County. There, he found a peaceful setting in which to build a cabin and set about a simple life that included reflection on his adventures and the largely solitary pathway of his existence. This book offers the stories that survived in his one remaining trunk, told with humor, insight, honesty—and the hard-won perspective gained from journeying and living fully.

*I love the dark hours of my being.
My mind deepens into them.
There I can find, as in old letters,
the days of my life, already lived,
and held like a legend, and understood.*

*Then the knowing comes: I can open
to another life that's wide and timeless.*

~ Rilke

I

Autobiography of a Misfit

I

Foreword

Autobiography of a Misfit

The object of this book is not to win fame. I am moved by a desire to record my eventful life with its possible social value, and register the manner of life of men I have met, admired, and cared for, with the conditions under which they lived, never again to be duplicated.

Also, I have a young son who by the laws of nature will not have my affection to guide him in his most impressionable years, and the conviction that, through his heritage of my instincts, it is going to be difficult for him to adjust himself to his environment. As I have experienced many of the trials with which he will be beset, I will chronicle the same; hand him my code in lieu of a better, and trust that thus ordained his life may be productive of worthier results; and failing in this, I at least may protect him from some of the unnecessary humiliation and physical discomforts I have endured.

If I partially succeed, then my work has been justified, and its influence may even extend to other misfits who find in the story something which will assist them in fulfilling their work without losing the consciousness that there are compensations in being different.

2

Childhood Days in England

In later life, it is difficult to decide how much of your childhood memories you have retained from your own observation, and how much is tradition. In my case I would ignore the traditional aspect because we were not that sort of family, and I have little recollection in the brief time I have been with them in these after years, that they ever lived in the past. Thus, much of home that I remember in the first four years of my life is due to my own reconstruction.

I was born, May 28th, 1868, in Richmond, Surrey, England, and my earliest recollection is that we lived in a large house at the foot of a very wide boulevard, which ran up a steep hill, and to my childish imagination, terminated three-quarters of a mile from home at the entrance of Richmond Park. Opposite this gate and across a large parade ground, stood the famous Star and Garter Hotel. All this hill I can nearly reconstruct. There were many affluent mansions surrounded by high brick walls on the right-hand side, and when you reached the top of the hill a high brick wall ran parallel to the road on the left-hand side, which enclosed the Park. The gates were five, the center one an enormous one, and arched with stone. Where any other road led, I know not. This was the only road of my memory and probably the one most often used.

Alan
family archive, editor

I could reconstruct much of the Park—with its glens and dales, and shadows and deer and my youthful imagination was capable of visualizing the gay cavalcades of the nobility of the past century who had traversed those wonderful aisles of oaks. I always pictured myself as a prominent figure, by no means the least in importance in these gay memories. I received, as my just dues the gratuitous acclamations, in my dreams, from a rabble consisting of the lesser breed who legitimately recognized us as superior mortals. Far was it at that time in my imagination, that I should fill a place in future life as one of that mob, and in such a position accept what was then to me an impossible heresy, that I was the equal of those on horseback.

My actual personal recollections have only one very distinct memory of that hill approaching the Park. At an early age, we were entrusted with iron-wire hoops and I remember we ran them down the hill until one time my eldest brother, gaining momentum from the grade, lost control of himself and the hoop, and violently swinging his arms tore his kneecap loose with the hook on the stick. The hoop with its own momentum struck a patient cab horse between the fore-legs, which was on stand by the curb. This was the only tragedy of my first four years of life. In future years I have wondered whether the cabman was fairly compensated and the horse cared for. I imagine at that time, with the intolerance of youth, the injury to man and horse was considered irrelevant and of no importance.

Of the house I only know it was large and the grounds extensive and surrounded by a high brick wall. The only building I have any clear memory of was a large one-story room in the extreme back corner of the walled grounds. This was used as a gymnasium and much of the guests' time and our own was devoted to practicing with foils which was then a fad.

Our summers were spent at the seashore in Dorsetshire in a cottage a half mile from the coast and standing alone on a large heath. What right my parents had to this place, I have no knowledge but as they kept it for years and it was named "Garry Cottage" after my mother's family, I assume they owned it.

Perhaps my recollection of Garry Cottage is aided by a picture of it painted by my mother, with a small boy in kilts in the foreground. As we grew we all persuaded ourselves that that small boy was a portrait of ourselves. On which one it was Mother would never commit herself so each was allowed to carry this honor to at least his own satisfaction. As we were all dressed at that time in Scotch Kilts the question is yet undecided.

Family archive, editor

My father was an Army Crammer which in England, was coaching young aristocrats to become officers in the army. Outside of my parents I have no strong recollections of persons in this period excepting a scrawny governess who burnt herself on my mind by her insistence on my learning the finger exercised on the piano.

At six I went to a boarding school called "Little St. Edmunds", which was situated I know not where. I remember much of the shape of the building. I remember the classroom was in a sub-cellar; that the headmaster's name was Moulton and that his sister who was elderly and stout acted as the housekeeper and carried with her a scent of lavender which not only advertised her presence but her passage. I remember trying to jump on a dare the ashes of a bonfire (the width of which is now mythical) and landing in the middle my shoes were filled with hot coals and I carry today the scar of the blisters.

Then some time in 1874 my Father appeared at the end of the term to take myself and my two elder brothers to a new home which was Brent Pelham Hall situated five miles from Buntingford Hertfordshire and ten miles from Bishop's Stortford.

What a treasure trove this house was to an imaginative child. An oblong brick building containing possibly thirty rooms, all of which, excepting the servant's quarters, were walled and ceiled in oak paneling—so ancient it was black as ebony. What promise those oak panels gave! How many thousands did we tap that a secret passage might be revealed or some hidden spring cabinet or panel which would disclose to us unheard of treasures? Alas! If the treasure is still there, it lays behind a panel we missed.

It was the manor house of the village of Brent Pelham *(leased from the Barclay Family)* and sat on a hill surrounded by acres of walled garden, while in the rear were woods, pasture and fields, which diversified to us children the range of exploration. The age of the house was probably two centuries and from modern standards it lacked every convenience, but to the small boy, his imagination could not picture a more ideal home.

Brent Pelham

The drive approaching the home was bordered by ancient yews, 40 feet high; the lawns rolled down to a road fringed by old poplar trees, and through this fringe we saw the church which appeared to us children as a mausoleum of the family who had owned the lands for centuries; to die out and leave their heritage to strangers. Through the kitchen garden ran an old moat, which had surrounded more ancient buildings than the ones then standing.

At the foot of the hill nestled the small village of Brent Pelham, and in the opposite direction, a quarter of a mile through a meadow, was the large swimming pond, ideally situated in the corner of one of the pastures, and bordered on two sides by woods.

To an English child at a public school, whose holidays at home consisted of six weeks in the summer; four weeks at Christmas and two weeks at Easter, here was an inexhaustible field of exploration stimulating to the wildest fancy.

In wet weather there were garrets, storerooms and cellars to be explored, their histories to be reconstructed; ghosts to be waylaid or relaid, and these pastimes gave our parents absolution from the necessity of entertaining us.

In finer weather there were the stables; the out-houses in the gardens; the rabbit warrens; the swimming hole, all calling; and when that day used to arrive when we were shipped back to school with one box of clothes and another of home cooked grub to mitigate the shock to a plainer regime, we knew that much of the next three months would be devoted to laying plans to further enlarging the joys of Brent Pelham.

How often my mind since those days has gone back to the old Hall and its associations. The days were never long enough: that wonderful old stairway and the feet my imagination put on it, the stained-glass window about 12 x 20 feet, lighting the black cavities of the hall from the first landing. The tenants with which I re-peopled the rooms, and the halls I filled with festive cavaliers and dames. If I ever had in my system a grain of calculation or prudence, here it was complete sterilized.

I cut an avenue 20 feet above ground through the yews, which made a complete passage from the lodge to the front door. Here I was brigand, highwayman, knight-errant, crusader-- everything that was adventurous and daring. I covered the church walls and floors with memorial tablets of my own heroic deeds in the defense of the oppressed and stricken; I wondered at the lack of imagination, or achievement of those already reposing in those sanctuaries and even had charitable thoughts for their spiritual peace of mind when I, with my exploits, encroached into their sphere. My parents furnished fuel to this form of romanticism by assuming the role of Lord and Lady Bountiful to the village. The Christmas holidays are memories of three great feeds given to the inhabitants: one to those over sixty, one to the middle aged and young couples, and one to the children. At each of these functions a Christmas tree featured with bales of corduroy pants and woolen petticoats for the adults and toys for the children, while the food and beer was prodigal. It was considered an act of grace that we children should assist at the waiting, but our true spiritual status was expressed by our eagerness with which we devoted ourselves to the liquid refreshments. It was more pleasing to our humor, and a response was much quicker arrived at, by pouring into the ever-empty glasses streams of beer, which for one day filled a year-old craving for all they could drink.

Alan, Charles, Ernest
Family archive, editor

So here we spent the holidays for five years. In the memories are stables; drives with Mother in the dogcart or Victoria; rare and much disliked visits to neighbours; and dogs—always dogs. There must have been thirty of them.

Then there were shoots in which we followed the gunmen, and the unforgettable picture of Mother teaching her three eldest sons to swim. We would walk or run across the fields a quarter of a mile to the swimming pond and change our clothes in a small bathhouse. The pond was probably forty yards long and it was over six feet at the deep end. Here we had a springboard and a ladder to climb the bank. None of us could swim when we went to Brent Pelham, but with Mother's, none too gentle tuition, we soon learnt. Her methods were decidedly Spartanic. She said she wished her boys to have both endurance and courage, and one of her methods to obtain this result was to take us out on the springboard and push us off. From the springboard when we came to the surface, she would shout instructions of how to get to the bank and the amount of fear your showed was the gauge with which she governed the time she thought it fit to come to your rescue. If you blubbered or showed panic, she would not consider that you needed aid until you had sunk a couple of times, but if you showed a disposition to rely on your own efforts she came in and gave you a shoulder to sustain you. With this form of teaching we learnt to swim quickly. This same pond also furnished us opportunity for a good deal of energy in boat building and for this pastime marvelous were the creations we laboriously manufactured.

It was at Brent Pelham that my eldest brother, Walter, was projected into a higher social status than ourselves, by Father presenting him with a horse of his own. Immediately he exercised a sort of thralldom over us which was productive in us being willing to be his hand-servant in return of a promise of a ride. For this reason, I and one of the keepers were beating a small grove of pines, one morning for rabbits, while Walter stood on the outskirts to shoot when they broke to freedom. A rabbit ran and Walter shot and I was in the line of fire, but fortunately standing at such a distance that the shot scarcely penetrated beneath the skin. My face was gaily speckled with the shots that had lodged, and Walter was overcome with remorse: how much with regard to myself and how much for fear of confiscation of his gun, I have never decided. The gardener with his knife dug out the pellets that had taken effect in my legs and face, and on the short walk to the house my worried brother was willing to give me a right in everything he possessed, including the pony. Here comes a fine point in the ethics of an English school boy. At least I know that fifty years ago if you lied, it was an unforgivable crime, which would completely ostracize you from your fellows, and no matter how severe the punishment to be avoided, it was seldom indulged in; but you were allowed to lie with chivalrous intention for the benefit of others.

My mind was made up that I would protect Walter in being held responsible. After washing the blood from my face, I went into the drawing room for that English function, "tea". My Grandmother who happened to be visiting us at that time seeing my face speckled like a dose of smallpox, asked me, what was the matter with my face. I replied, "I fell down."

She looked again and said, "Why it would be impossible to make all those little spots by falling down."

This was crowding my resources and I sullenly replied, "I fell down."

Dear Grandmother who among other virtues abominated anything that savored of sneakiness curled one side of her nose—a habit which she had when she sensed an offense, and said, "But Alan, you couldn't make scars like that by falling down."

I repeated still more sullenly, "I fell down."

This in no way satisfied my Grandmother who was going to continue the inquisition, when my Mother with the intuition which has caused her sons to reverence her memory, undoubtedly decided that I was lying, and intended to lie, and maybe that I was justified in lying, and she looked up and said, "Mother, let him alone."

The incident was closed; my face remained scarred for days but I was never asked for an explanation.

Strange I can never reconstruct to my own satisfaction the passage way between the kitchen and the front of the house. To arrive in the kitchen, I have to leave one of the front doors, and swing into the grove which surrounded the well that was dug by hand 180 feet deep. The water from this well was raised to tanks on the top of the house by four labourers working the rotary wheels for an hour each day. From the well I followed a path to the kennels where I perhaps lingered with the kennel-man, whose duties were caring for the pack of about twenty-five beagles kept to run hares; and he was also custodian of the various individually owned dogs (of which each member of the household considered him or herself entitled to one or more), and after looking over the well-built quarters and runs, watching a feeding, and seriously discussing some remedy for mange or itch or other canine disease, you left through the stable yard, passed the chicken corrals and thus to the back door.

The entrance was really through a dark outhouse which was the home bakery and contained a great brick oven, twelve feet in length, and if you were weary of the thrill of crawling through its small door and going to the end and back, you continued twenty feet up a dark passage at the end of which, taking a left hand turn of a few feet, brought you to the kitchen. The right turn took you into the (to us taboo) servants' quarters, which taboo was generally respected. I had to feel years later a real hunger myself, before I speculated any on why, when, where and what the servants of that house ate. The only clear memory I have is that after the hour of eleven beer flowed until lunch, and you could then meet the various employees, either making their way to the kitchen which was the dispensing point—or already there!

The stable was a large one and above the stalls was a loft to keep hay. To get to the loft you went into the harness room, which was twenty-five feet high and contained a stairway so steep as to be almost a ladder, which ended in a platform giving entrance to the loft. One day—probably on account of rain—I had been amusing myself by throwing down hay, and tiring of this way of annoying the grooms, I was swinging in the handrail of the platform when it broke. I landed posterior down in a startled bunch of men cleaning harness around the stove. Fate perversely caused me to strike the stove with my heels as I catapulted onto the brick hearth. The result was a fractured pelvis bone which acts today as a barometer, but at the time the paramount issue was to keep the parents from knowing about it, as I was under a temporary injunction to stay away from the stables. Binding the grooms to secrecy, I succeeded in dragging around in a sufficiently upright posture for the next week to convince the elders that I was suffering from nothing worse than a severe jolt due to an ordinary tumble, and if it were not for the occasionally rheumatic twinges in these latter years, the experience would have been forgotten in a few weeks.

When I was somewhere between the age of seven and eight, I was taken away from Little St. Edmund's and placed in a boarding school in London. This school in Bayswater, was kept by two elderly sisters who were, according to my parents expected to exercise a beneficent feminine influence, as I was given to understand that I was becoming too rowdy.

If my parents had consulted any of the twenty boys who were captives in this reconverted residence, they would have found that this petticoat government was more harsh that they would imagine it to be from the sex of the principals, who gave more attention to extracting a living from a vocation they disliked, than they gave to exercising a charm on the pupils. Their personality was not one that would win affection from a child, and their punishments, when too severe for their strength were administered by a brother who had some sort of periodic employment in the city that caused him to disappear for days at a time.

The only concession that was made to a boy's craving for games was a fives court in the backyard, and a vigorous drill for two hours each week from an ex-sergeant of infantry. All the other exercise we gained, was long, aimless walks in the afternoons, when in squad formation; forbidden to break line or step, we walked miles to some place we did not want to get and back again.

Mother in some manner found time to write to all of her sons once a week when we were away from home, and these letters gave us some little prestige among the other boys because she had no little skill drawing and a ready wit and they were illustrated with symbols wherever they could be made to take the place of words and their receipt was quite an event with us. We would attempt to emulate her example in reply but I suspect they were unintelligible.

The Deanery at Westminster in Dean Stanley's time

By special concession, my younger brother, Ernest and I were permitted to spend occasional days with friends. This gave us some Sundays with our Grandmother who had a home in Chelsea, and others we spent with a friend of Father's, Dean Stanley, who was in charge of the Abbey and school at Westminster. These Sundays in the Abbey made a very lasting impression on my mind, and I became well acquainted with all the historic features of that huge monument. Not the least of my pleasures was listening, during the services, to the magnificent choir of young voices – trained from Westminster school— which in those great domes, it was almost easy for me to persuade myself was celestial melody. These days of quiet peace, with the lunch and tea taken with the Dean and his sister at the Deanery, form one of many permanently pleasant memories.

The days spent with our Grandmother had a somewhat different flavor, but equally quiet. She was inclined to be religious and lived a calm life wherein her material welfare was perfectly and unassumingly ministered to by two faultless servants. If it were Sunday, we attended a morning service. After lunch, at which our tastes were catered to in small delicacies, we would probably be asked to read a chapter of the Bible and comment on it. Then tea and a cab back to school.

Across the road from the school was a large common in one corner of which was an ambitious church called St. Augustine *(Kilburn Park Rd)*, and this was the official place of worship of the ladies who were our moral mentors. It had a full surplice choir, with ceremonies that were almost pontifical in their magnificence, and before I had been two years under the new order, I became a choir boy.

As a child I was impressionable, and I think at no time was I more sublimated than when parading around the aisles following the swinging incense. I would sing with a concentrated fervor that would suggest that my salvation depended on my effort.

I had been what might be termed a "boyish boy". I was nicknamed, "Pug", named not after a prizefight but after a species of canine, and I had in a humble manner attempted to make my cognomen appropriate. This mood was passing—I was becoming religious; my hero, Richard Coeur de Leon, had made way for Cardinal Wolsey.

I found it difficult to abandon the mailed fist in just one imaginative flight, as my training had all trended to convince me that spiritual food was more palatable to the mob when delivered to them by an injunction, but even that trace of belligerency passed; I became decided that spiritual salvation of the mass was in ourselves. Each individual must work out his life through self-denial. Monks became to be the holiest of men and I planned a future life in an ascetic brotherhood.

St. Augustine displaced Wolsey and became my patron saint. I felt the necessity to bring my unpopular conviction to the other boys and prove by example that I was sincere. I gave up the indulgences of my past misspent life, which had mostly been debauches (when I had the money) at the pastry cook's. I made myself amiable in duties to my fellows as my conscience suggested. I kept fast days, wore a crucifix, and read the Bible when I felt the knowing of more energetic impulses; I entertained visions of missionary work among wild races and service of sacrifice in leper colonies; I built an oratory for my own devotions in the school dormitory so that there could be no shadow of doubt of my conversion, and as an example to the benighted heathens who refused to respect my faith.

This frame of mind lasted for a year and it brought me a certain fame. I sincerely allowed myself to be used by the ladies of the house as a lure to the parents of prospective pupils and helped to convince them that any tough kid could be brought to the same condition of spiritual excellence under their tuition.

As I carried my helpful disposition and mild manners wherever I went my fame as a "nice boy" extended beyond the school; and the only person in whom I sensed any doubt of my improved state was my Mother. Although she made no attempt to change my habits, if I tried to involve her in a spiritual discussion, she looked at me as if speculating on the probable beneficial effects of a dose of Gregory Powder. By after deduction I am positive she did not think I was acting as a normal boy should.

I don't know what was the cause of me falling from grace—probably from a worldly sincerity in one of my self-appointed apostles, or the conviction of a basic gold standard in religion—but at nine I was, according to the ladies of the school, in a more godless state than when I first saw the light. The "nice boy" who had formerly been asked to tea in the sitting room when visitors came was now allowed to continue his play in the school-yard uninterrupted. They began to make suggestions that it would not offend them if my parents would remove me to another sphere of scholarship.

Without being sensible of hypocrisy, my position as star in the play had compensated me for all my sacrifice.

In retrospect of fifty years, I see in this incident the same influence which has dominated every event of my life. I think I have a passion for truth; but somewhere in my subconscious mind is an irresistible urge, which causes me to make gestures that are unexpected. I find that this impulse has controlled my life and made it to be a record of decisions which were startling and imprudent.

Once having been convinced in my conscious mind that a suggested course was not distasteful to my code, the subconscious has rounded the desire into action regardless of the price to myself, when any other individual, if placed in a similar position, and not equipped with this secret urge to be different -- would condemn the performance as ill-considered and abnormal.

It was late in life when I discovered and classified this powerful factor in my fate and through this ignorance I have made no struggle to protect myself against its Influence, and the consequence was that existence has been a long series of losing battles, -- the scars of which I carry with no little pride.

My condition for the next few months was not a happy one. Nobody liked me. My fellow pupils had disapproved of me in my position as a model, and now they inconsistently resented my return to their ranks as another reflection upon myself. In the holidays my Father and Mother also showed disappointment at my attitude. They both had a pronounced and sincere faith, and although they had been surprised, and a little alarmed at my excessive enthusiasm for religion, they resented my showing no evidence of any faith whatsoever. This led to a partial estrangement which caused me, both at home at the school to become more dependent on entertaining myself, and I became a greedy reader of all the adventurous forms of literature that I could lay my hands upon, and it is unfortunate that most of it was very cheap trash.

In England in the seventies (1870's), there was a flood of adventure stuff which was easily procurable at a very small price and I became saturated with wild tales of piratical adventures on all the seas of the earth. I began to live in those adventures myself: Buccaneer Moors, murderous Malays; Piratical Chinese, seemed more familiar to me than the maid who served the meals.

I had come to another decision; as a citizen of the world I was lost. My destiny was to become a pirate. To me it was only a matter of a few preliminary details of getting to the dock. My farewells to civilization were going to give me no grief. They did not appreciate me anywhere, and I took a satisfaction in feeling that when they next heard of me, it would be through some particularly atrocious set of rapine or blood lust which would at least excite their fear.

The next question was how to get to the ship. I knew that ships would be found in the docks, and the docks were on the Eastside of London. It seemed very reasonable to me that if I could find a ship I could select a pirate; having found the pirate I was satisfied with my own ability to fight to the command. Then with one blood-thirsty exploit I should be vindicated before my parents and school fellows.

I had one doubt—the story of Saul and Jonathan had always impressed me. I needed a chief mate that I could trust implicitly, and preferably bound by a blood-bond. My poor brother Ernest was selected.

Taking him aside one night, I told him what the fortunes had in store for him. Although he was a little astonished, he said he'd be prepared to leave next morning at eight.

Eight o'clock, according to schedule, after eluding the school servants, we were outside the gate and headed in a general easterly direction. We had made no preparations, as I expected to be fed and clothed when making contact with the pirate crew. In our hurried exit we had even forgotten to lace our shoes but this was remedied when two or three blocks on the road to freedom.

We walked without daring to ask for directions until nearly three o'clock. I had been for some time noticing in my brother a very unpiratical inclination to sniffle! This filled me with disgust. I had no tenderness with his eight years of inexperience, or his lack of a literary foundation for a life of piracy; sympathy among pirates was a vice. Was this material that I could trust when I sent him on an errand murderous and bloody? No! My confidence had been betrayed. I had a chief mate to give away. I couldn't use him.

In my dilemma of how to get rid of him, by some freaky coincidence, I discovered that we were on the street in which our Grandmother lived. Eureka! I would shake the weak. After comforting him into coherency, I pointed him out Grandmother's door and told him to go and ring the bell, which under the promise of food, he cheerfully did. I stood at the corner of the street until I saw the maid open the door, and then freed from my last encumbrance of civilization I cheerfully turned toward the open seas.

I had no uncertainty, that I should be accepted as a blood brother on any pirate ship I attempted to join forces with, but I intended to exercise caution in my selection. There was the fine point to be considered, of a quick rise to command, and I also had not yet made up my mind in which branch of the industry I would devote my energies. The choice was so delightfully varied, and I was hesitating whether it would be smuggling in Africa; silk on the Morocco coast; Junks in the China seas; merchant men around Malay, or gold from Peru.

What was my horror and indignation when I found myself struggling with a panting and excited maid. Was the future pirate captain going to be ruined by a woman? Nay, nay! I fought, but was mortified to find that I could not break her grip on my arm. My brother without regard to the wreck of my future prospects had sobbed his tale to my Grandmother and she had had the presence of mind to immediately dispatch a maid to cut off my career by bringing me back herself, or if unable, to call a policeman. Never had my pride been so hurt. I would not go back with her. If a policeman – well, then a policeman; and I was led back by the police a captive.

The next scene was the policeman taking Ernest and myself back to school in a cab. Then several floggings. I had been used to the severest forms of the rather severe whippings which English schools considered part of the curriculum, but this was the worst I had encountered. The brother of the proprietor was sent for from the city, and he did the thrashing, and each time I was whipped I was told of the enormity of my offense, -- I had ruined his sisters and disgraced the school by giving it the reputation of a place that boys ran away from. I was told that I was expelled, and that they were only awaiting my Father to take me home. In this was some comfort.

When my Father arrived I was sullen and resentful at the treatment I had received, but happy at the thought that Brent Pelham was the end of the journey.

My parents scolded me, but not inordinately; Mother asked me to tell her the story, which I did. Although she did not smile or comment favorably, I sensed a certain sympathy for my point of view, or at least for the spirit involved, and this seemed to demonstrate itself by her consideration of my obvious loneliness. We took long walks with the dogs in the woods, during which she probably pumped me dry of all my ideals, while apparently instructing in bird and game lore. These confidential chats with that Mother of mine have always been a dear memory. She had the ability of reducing herself to a child's age and a child's standards, in a manner which carried a conviction of comprehension.

After several weeks at home my parents found a place for me on the HMS the *Worcester*, which was a training ship for officers in England's Mercantile Marine under the patronage of the Navy and was anchored off Greenhithe in the Thames River.

The minimum age for admission to this school was twelve years and I was but ten years of age, but by some influence this obstacle was overcome. I was launched on a maritime career. Why this branch of the service was selected for me I have always been in some doubt. It may have been from a suggestion they had gathered from my interest in sea stories and traveling, but it more probably was the conviction that the naval discipline under which the ship was run would be beneficial to my somewhat unruly temperament.

To arrive at the *Worcester* you took train from London to Greenhithe, then a quarter of a mile walk and you came to the small village which sat on the bank of the Thames. The *Worcester*, anchored fore and aft, was a half mile from the pier; an old converted three-decker, 72 gun frigate, equipped as a full rigged ship.

HMS Worcester

I arrived on board in a boat rowed by the cadets and climbed a gangway up her tall side. I had become a unit of England's great maritime power.

The work on board was entirely done by the cadets with the exception of the cooking, sick-bays and laundry, all other work falling to our duties: scrubbing, washing, sweeping, bed making, or (rather as we slept in hammocks, hammock making) were in the day. The hammocks were slung each evening in regular drill, and unslung and stored in racks in the morning to clear the sleeping deck of all suggestion of its nocturnal use. Everything was performed under a rigid (but not excessively harsh) naval discipline.

The six classes headed by six different masters covered mathematics, geography, nautical astronomy and navigation; and to this we gave five hours a day. After graduating from the *Worcester* a cadet was qualified to pass a full master's examination in these subjects, and the only barrier between him and a command was the actual time experience, which the law demanded, on a sea-going ship.

There were also six seamanship and drill instructors which had been recruited from pensioned able-seaman of the Navy. These men covered all the manual instruction of seamanship and taught us to knot, splice, set and furl sails and to completely rig and unrig a ship.

Saturday afternoons we played ashore in a field belonging to the ship, and we practiced many forms of athletics in a gymnasium on board.

We wore at all duties on board, an undressed sailor's uniform, (cotton in summer and serge in winter) and for shore leave, or what we called "liberty", we had a very attractive adaptation of a naval midshipman's uniform and the bold buttons, gold lace and the gold embroidered cap gave us a very smart appearance in which we took no little pride.

Alan R. Hiley as Worcester cadet
ARH archive, editor

The two hundred pupils were divided into watches and officered by those of us who had shown efficiency enough to attract attention of the Captain or the chief officer. These billets were eagerly sought as they carried many privileges dear to a youngster. There were less duties; more independence more gold lace, and considerable personal authority attached to the honor, and the kid that became "Captain of the Foretop", or "Captain of the Mizzentop", was expected by his school fellows to swagger; and did.

In going to the *Worcester*, I imagine in a sense I was filling a certain family tradition. I don't believe any of my family had ever been in commerce, and the nearest I had ever heard of their contact with it, was that my Grandfather (Forbes in Edinburgh) had been a banker which to our minds was a little derogatory. By all standards of our family ethics, only the Army, Navy or Church furnished the orthodox and suitable vocations. The *Worcester* trained for the Marine Service, but you could call for an acceptance as an officer of the Navy, and perhaps my parents had a hope that I would do so. My last experience in the religious field had undoubtedly convinced them that I was not the most suitable selection for the church, and Walter, the eldest, by right of entail, had already selected the Army as his prerogative.

Sometime during the first year I was on the *Worcester*, my parents moved again; this time to Hyde Hall, close to the village of Sawbridgeworth. This large house was the seat, or one of the seats, of the Earl of Roden and was considerably more spacious that Brent Pelham, containing at least twenty-five guest rooms with adequate quarters to cater to this form of household.

Hyde Hall, Sawbridgeworth, England
historic photo

The house was magnificently situated on the top of a hill with large grounds laid to gardens, with artificial ponds. The whole was surrounded by fifty acres of meadow and woods.

In the valley at the foot of the hill was the railroad station and a half mile beyond was the village to which Hyde Hall was the manor house.

I have no conception of why the move was made. *(ed.: according to Barclay the considerable noise of train activity next door may have been reason).* Both my parents, I have since learned, had some money and probably at that time my Mother was comparatively well-off. I think they were largely influenced in their selection of a bigger house by a desire to extend my Father's scope as a coach for the Army. The house now contained several pupils of the richest and most influential families of England, and the comforts and accommodations at Brent Pelham had doubtless become unsatisfactory.

A child's heart is seldom a very loyal one, and Brent Pelham was soon put aside for the new and unknown. Gardens, greenhouses, stables, kennels and fields had to be all familiarized.

The gardens were well cared for and the hothouses contained grapes, while plums, apricots and peaches were trained on the south side of the kitchen garden walls. There was a large orchard of gnarled apple trees which were familiar to us because they sheltered the archery range between the rows. They certainly produced no fruit that was edible raw, and with acres of trees we got our eating apples from America by the barrel.

We were now in a more settled community than at Brent Pelham and there was more social life, which was in evidence by garden parties, and dinners, with once a year a formal ball. Then there were often visits from the parents of the young men who were under Father's tuition, and persons of national fame were often among the guests. This scarcely impressed the minds of us boys who took it as a matter of course, but we were grateful for the tennis courts which came in the train of all this hospitality. The visiting list was in no way a free one. The house contained many of the most eligible young men in England, so the guests were limited most exclusively to the country gentry or other elite.

The servants were practically the same that I had always known, and seemed to take each move of the family as appropriate. There was Bah Howland who nursed Mother's seven children, Burls, the butler, who had for eighteen years waited for Bah to be released from her duties so that they could marry; Sarah, the cook; and Eliza the chief housemaid; Stone the coachman, all aided in making each new house appear to us as home. There were probably twenty people catering to the comfort of the family and its guests. How and what they were paid, I never have known.

As far as I am concerned I can never remember money (in the sense of procuring money) ever being discussed. The necessities, food and raiment, were ordered and came. There was always an abundance of the best, and everybody, including the servants, accepted this as the natural course of events. This in no way implies that there was extravagance or any vain display. The family food was plainer and infinitely more wholesome than the average American business man considers becoming, and I think I can remember to this day most of the gowns that my Mother wore in the years of this period. For actual cash, we boys were given five dollars each school term which had to last us for four months and the holiday gratuities would probably average twenty-five cents a week. Two cents spent in candy, we considered an indulgence, four cents spent in the same way would be gluttony. A tennis racquet; a cricket ball or bat, such as these, by judicious representation, could be procured. Had we felt inclined to nurse a secret vice, it would have starved to death.

In this home, many of those great in England's counsels today, finished their education, and if I have at any time forgotten or minimized the charm which my Father and Mother exercised beyond their family circle, I am reminded of their grace by the testimony of their admirers. I wonder how often Sir Henry Rawlinson, the Duke of Westminster, Prince Francis of Teck, (the Queen's brother), the Duke of St Albans, Lord Hawke, Sir Robert Peel, Albert Baillie, James Baillie, Farrar, and many others go back with pleasant reminiscences of Hyde Hall and its associations.

From the standard of happiness, few boys have been so blessed as to have such a home as ourselves. Provided we observed certain unwritten laws of truth, cleanliness and abstinence in eating, we were allowed to pursue our own pleasure without severe rebuke.

In the winter there was skating on the artificial ponds, rabbit hunting with ferrets, and fishing in our own or local ponds, and we gained some skill in landing twelve to twenty-pound pike, which is one of the gamiest fish on earth.

In summer there was bathing and boating. We kept our own boathouse on the River Stort, which was also utilized as a bathhouse, and we became adepts in many forms of outdoor sport.

The test that we used as proficiency in swimming, (and also nerve) was to open the lock gates and while the water was rushing in, dive through the sluiceway. We had no scruples, while preparing an initiate for trial, in drawing on our imaginations for stories of those who had hung in the gate of this three-foot raceway with a ten-foot enclosed vertical drop. This pastime was one of the few that had not parental sanction.

On many excursions Mother was not only our companion, but one of us. Swimming, skating or boating she was skilled in, and with what pride I can now visualize her (a mother of seven children) playing tennis single-handed and beating two of the best of us, and then, as the game was finished and we adjourned for tea, she in a glorious stride of health, would take the back of a garden chair in a running jump.

Don't think from these notes that we were co-educationalist or even co-players. Women and girls were an entirely different breed. Mother with her bobbed hair and short skirts (this in 1875) had redeemed herself and was thus to be honored: and was. The only other exception that we made was our eldest sister (Sybil) who was now of an age in which she could not be ignored, and from her loneliness, excited our magnanimous masculine pity. To show our generosity when she joined our sports, we hazed her with more cruelty than we would have used toward a stranger of our own sex. She had to show her qualification to be accepted as an equal. When she played hockey with us on the ice, we would deliberately skate into her when she was in no way obstructing the play, and she had to appear satisfied with a similar grueling in all our pastimes. What nice little animals!

I must bear witness that she never wilted and qualified as a stayer and good sport. I wonder how much this training has influenced her life? She is still a spinster, living on a small income in a small English village. Still active and athletic, and her joy, is boyish boys, and all they stand for when wholesome. *(according to Peter Hiley, for a while she happily ran a boarding house in London for young men lodgers. She helped her brother Ranald in Australia for awhile, was close to his daughter her namesake Sibyl. Ed.)*

Here I want to record two incidents which happened about this time. They have always been tender spots on my pride, but they are illustrative of Mother's genius and had a great deal to do with influencing my actions in life.

Ordinary rain made little difference to us and wet clothes or wet shoes were seldom changed before the evening meal, and in winter, from playing and wading in slush and snow, we suffered considerably from chilblains.

My two elder brothers and I had been constructing a snowman on one of the walks outside the house. My hands becoming chilled, and wanting to warm them, I went into the library where Mother was sitting. She did not look up from her book, but as I held my hands to the fire, I thought their chapped condition demanded a little sympathy and I gave a "b-r-r-r" to attract attention. "What is the matter, Alan?" she asked.

"My hands are cold."

"Where are your brothers?"

"Outside making a snowman."

"Go on out."

I went. I vowed a thousand times since that no one should call me a quitter again.

The other example: A pupil of Father's had given me a three-penny bit (six cents), and in the pride of my wealth I confided the fact to Mother. I was instructed to return it with the message that I had made a mistake in accepting it, and the donor had made a mistake in offering it. Several times since, I have been hungry enough to beg food. This memory has made it easier to pull up my belt a couple of holes.

Our evenings at home were often spent in reading aloud, but the family, including Grandmother, were keen chess enthusiasts, and we had our handicaps graded according to proficiency in past performances and there was generally one game going. Then Mother, who had some talent, both in singing and playing, would at periods gather us around the piano and we would sing popular ballads, preferably Scotch, or hymns. On stormy nights while the wind howled outside, as was fitting in a maritime country whose history was founded on "those who go down to the sea in ships: we would bawl with all our heart:

"O Lord, we cry to thee

For those in peril on the sea."

To us children there were few social obligations. We were expected to be on time for breakfast because tardiness denoted laziness, at lunch we were allowed a little more latitude because we might be legitimately delayed, but at dinner we had to be exactly on time. We had to be punctual for Sunday morning service in the church and also the more or less state occasions of the village entertainments gotten up by local talent, such as bazaars and concerts of a community nature. This was our total tribute to Caesar.

When there was company in the drawing room or any but young people in the grounds, we had occupations elsewhere. If the persons visiting happened to have qualified to our standard of fame, we would from curiosity make an opportunity to see if their appearances bore out their reputation.

Mother was not immune from pride in her five boys and on some occasions, either in response to a request or vanity, a servant was sent to round us up and inform us that we were wanted in the drawing room. This was unwelcome but a command, and we left our pursuits and trooped in to comply, carrying in our bearing evidence that we did not approve of the interruption.

We were all together too masculine and too disheveled to excite many feminine rhapsodies, particularly if the critic was a timid one, but the youngest, Ranald, who was delicate and ethereal and nearly always clean, invariably saved the situation. The embarrassed visitor running her eye over four sullen faces would finally let it rest on Ranald and exclaim, "What a dear little boy!"

This was the prelude to dismissal, and release to all but Ranald. The moment the door was closed behind us we would attempt to give an illustration and use him for a subject on how much we ourselves appreciated, "dear little boys, pretty little boys." He was hugged, muzzled and kneaded until he attracted attention by crying or we tired of the sport.

Walter Jr., Rev.Walter Hiley, Sybil, Ranald, Henrietta Jemima Forbes, Frances "Dolly", Ernest, Charles, Alan, Laddie
family archives, editor

On the *Worcester*, although the life was more restrained, it was not an unhappy one. For a healthy child the variety of pastimes were always stimulating and competition in achievement gave our energies a large scope.

We had every form of boat racing from four-oared gigs to twenty-four-oared cutters, and on account of our profession the sports we took the greatest interest in were aquatic. I seemed not to be handicapped by being two years younger than any of the other boys.

Our life was very full and laying as we did at the mouth of the largest port in the world, there was a constant stream of passing ships.

If it were clear we would discuss their firms, destinations and sailing qualities, and if it were foggy, we were still conscious that the traffic was in no way abated as we heard the sirens of the tugs which hurried them either to the dock or the open sea. P&O boats from India; clipper ships to Australia; Donald Curries to the cape; all were catering to the spirit of a venturesome race; all carried human freights who were seeking or returning from fortune. And the least in the vision of these wayfarers was the actual cash involved.

Many of the ships officered by past *Worcester* Cadets, dipped their ensign in salute, and after having received a reply, signaled greetings and identification. And we, still land-bound, fell dreaming to our future commands. Was it a wonder that few of us developed much practicability? We lived in dreams; pawing over maps and building empires on those parts of them that had the fewest names inscribed.

Thus two years passed, during which I began to take a lead in the school affairs and was keen on the spirit involved. My life was so full that it seemed sufficient, when I was startled from my conception of any established order by a summons to come home. My Mother was dead.

The way across London to home was a long one. Mother to us had appeared so much alive that it seemed impossible that she could be dead. How had it happened? We had heard of an athletic heart which had curtailed violent exercises, but for this to have killed her was unreasonable. Then there were horses of which she had been warned, but this solution I did not want to accept.

Youth at twelve is callous to an ordinary death, but Mother had seemed a permanency and the change was incomprehensible. Mother was the only strong attraction I had. She had my absolute respect which is a child's equivalent to love. She was the only critic I feared and the only judgment I considered above question.

When I arrived home, I found a broken house. Mother had died violently by falling through a skylight. For years everybody had used a heavy glass skylight to walk on when going to the flat roof. This time it broke and Mother—who with some young people were looking for a wasp's nest—crashed to the hall below.

This was my first contact with death and a child never understands it the first time, even in the case of his own Mother. The realization comes later, and it was years before I understood the significance of what had happened. How could I know then that I had lost my only conscious spiritual director, and that I was to wander lonely years searching for the contact I had lost.

To a family so avowedly stoic as ourselves the unrestrained grief was bound to make an impression on my mind, and the respect and affection from hundreds in all parts of England was a matter of sly pride to me, but the keyed emotional pitch was overbearing, and it was a relief when she was laid away in the village church yard. Since then I know she was, and is, my inspiration to cleanliness, and I have made some effort to follow her standards in my life. Much I have done of which she would not approve, particularly with women, but largely she is what has kept my head above water. If I believed in a future life, and expected to reach a spiritual world, it would be in her judgement and commendation I would be most interested.

It was from the extensive death notices that I first learnt of the importance of our own family. I had always known we were of a "good family" and our conduct had been gauged by what was fitting behavior to those so born, but I did not know that biologically I was as near a thorough-bred as occurs among humans. Grandmother was the last lineal descendant of the Lords of the Isles, tracing progenitors in direct succession to the years 1060 and then by legend and fable to Fingal about 300 A.D., and these chiefs owning all of the world they desired, had not been influenced in marriage by any law than selecting mothers of chiefs to come. No wonder we had always been impressed that lying or cheating was not for us, but for those who careless of themselves, could besmirch nothing but themselves. And here was another field of romance opened for me, and I had never before heard of it. Father's family only went back to the Crusaders and sank immediately into comparative insignificance. I adopted the MacDonalds as my legitimate inheritance and I think with some justification. My instincts leaned to a lawless state, and feeling above the law I have often tried to imitate the clan's elite in making my own. And such a one I think my Mother was, who in her decisions often flaunted public opinion, as instance, her bobbed hair for convenience; and today, forty-five years later, I appreciate her not so much as my Mother, but as a mother who desired her children above the flesh.

In ten days I was back on the *Worcester*, but something had happened—I was in revolt. I could reason sufficiently clearly to recognize I could not avoid the authority which controlled me, but I found I could influence it to change. A mandate suggested to my mind a question mark, and I met the distasteful ones with a restricted resistance which was productive (on the same principle as water wears stone) in results. I became conscious that the written law was not infallible.

This attitude both at home and on the *Worcester* caused a different scale of values. I received a greater measure of indulgences, and was given a certain status as a leader. As I endeavoured never to propound a question that was illogical, I was generally accepted (when the argument was not altogether unorthodox) as worthy of consideration by my antagonist. Ah me! David and Goliath.

This does not mean that I mutinied or was in open defiance. My method was more subtle than that, I was precocious but not unwitty. I became a favorite with Captain Smith and Mr. Buck, the head master; and I frequently went to tea with the masters who lived in villas ashore and acquired much privilege thereby.

After my Mother's death I had worked and obtained the petty-officership of "Captain of the Foretop" and scarcely had I reached this rank when I saw better fields for my talent. There was a ranking named, "Captain of the Signals" and the duties of this berth were to remain on the poop, and take charge of all the duties of the semi fore and flag signaling. The incumbent of this berth had two cadets under him and had extraordinary privileges which included a wonderful design of gold embroidered flags to be worn on his dress uniform; the coxswainship of the Captain's six-oared gig, absolution from all drills, and the use of the deckhouse with its signal lockers, easy chairs, lounges, and reading matter. And the consideration of being the one boy that was directly in contact with the powers. No other boy except myself and assistants were allowed on the poop. In this rank I was in a position to meet intimately the Captain's guests, and met many famous people, among which my strongest recollections are of Princess Louise, one of Queen Victoria's daughters and Rosa Bonheur whose chum she was. They would come down on the *Worcester* on weekends to paint.

The Captain has a custom when he and his wife had guests to dinner of asking or commanding the presence of one or more of the boys, which was an honor valued as a recognition of efficiency, and if on such occasions I had been overlooked by any mistake, it was quite within the scope of my nerve to cheekily quiz the Captain on the wherefore. The food was a consideration to a boy that meant a treat.

Today I am confident that Captain Smith in his heart gave me more affection than he allowed himself to show any other cadet. I might even deduce that being himself childless, he regarded me as approaching his idea of what he would like a son to be. I know he allowed himself intimacies which one would hardly suspect in him when he paraded in full dress uniform down the drill lines.

There was a system on the quay ashore for signaling any message, or calling a boat, and there was constant traffic coming to and fro, carrying passengers and freight, the custom being that the delivery man for the butcher, the baker and candlestick maker would leave his order on our back porch a quarter of a mile away and signal the fact to the ship, and there was always a ship's boat and a signal man attending to this duty.

In the Captain's cabins, which were quite spacious, there was a long balcony conservatory which extended around the stern of the ship, and the old gun ports in his saloon had been fitted to represent greenhouses and contained imitation grape vines on which were clusters of wax grapes. The Captain was very proud of these, but my standard of austere criticism which rejected anything so obviously artificial, forced me in my conception of honesty to occasionally use them as a vehicle of wit, which knowing the Captain's pride, offended good taste. Today I have come to the realization that to him that make-believe was only a palliative in lieu of an impossible reality. Every seaman's dream is a picture of an old age in a cottage with a garden, and a floor that doesn't heave, and here was poor Captain Smith retired from sea, but doomed to still walk a deck. His vineyard was his expression of a hope which had died.

There was a change going on in my moral outlook at this time. I had not altered my conviction that females were the inferior of males, but I spent more time speculating on the sex. Unfortunately, smutty books were easily obtainable and were current among the boys. The secrecy with which these books were passed around is now, and was then, an affront to my sense of outright-ness, but the intense curiosity made me sacrifice principles. To get a copy of this garbage you would act with as much cunning as if you were a conspirator to assassinate the Queen. To the boys making a transfer, shame made the very walls have eyes.

It is sad this traffic could not be killed in a school by ordinary honesty in meeting an enquiring mind on the threshold. The squeamishness of the Victorian era has been responsible for many regrets, and much of mine. One would imagine, if for no other reason, a pride of race would have forced an enlightenment in English schools.

3

The Day the Admiralty Called

HMS Worcester
historic photo

Once every year the HMS *Worcester*, as a protégé of the Navy was inspected by the Lords of the Admiralty, and this was an occasion of more than usual smartness. The guns which stood on the upper deck were oiled and polished so that they looked like reflectors: the brass work was rubbed and the decks scrubbed and scoured with holystone bricks until they were immaculate. It was The Day of the year, and every rope yarn was picked up and ropes coiled so there could no reproach for a lack of neatness.

Along each yard aloft about four feet above the yard, were stretched guy-lines, and the boys would use these as a balance to walk out on the spars. When each spar had received its quota the boys would lock arms and form the manoeuvre called, "manning yards." To see a full-rigged ship with horizontal yards completely decorated with lines of human figures dressed in spotless white duck was a very impressive and beautiful sight. I have often wondered since, that there were no accidents while practicing this drill because some of the yards were one hundred feet above the deck and before the order was given to "dress" there was a good deal of rough skylarking.

In my twelfth year it fell to my lot to be coxswain of the gig which was to bring the Admiralty from the shore, and this was the greatest honor for recognition of efficiency, that any boy could win. For several days before the date set for the great event, we devoted much time to cleaning the gig in which we would fetch on board the *Worcester* the representatives of what we considered the most potential authority in England. Our boat, a six-oared gig was in perfect shape, and a thing of beauty --- long, narrow and swift. On each end were airtight compartments covered with wooden gratings and these we holystoned white; the rudder yoke and the oar rowlocks were brass, which we polished; and the tiller ropes of white cotton cord were pipeclayed to make them whiter. The tiller ropes ran through a complicated set of pulleys which had no use except as an ornamental effect, making an elaborate design on, and above, the after-grating. In all she was the fastest and smartest gig on the river and her coxswain, not to mention the crew, was proud of her.

We went ashore in ample time, and moored fore and aft to the quay. By some freak of fate I happened to be in funds, and made reckless with the honor thrust on me, I took the crew up to the village to treat them at the bakery. At that time there were two delicacies for which we craved: one was a sixpenny can of condensed milk in which, for perfect enjoyment we would punch two small holes with our marling spike, and assimilate the contents by suction; the other was a tuppenny tart, which was what an American would call a "pie" and retailed at the cost of four cents. One on most occasions was a ration to a boy, but in cases of extraordinary hospitality, such as this, two were well within his limit. We stayed up in the village until we saw coming from the depot a bevy of men dressed in silk hats and frock coats and this we knew was our party, as English officers in the Navy and Army wore mufti in travel. We ran down to the boat ahead of them: untied the mooring lines, got out the boat-hooks, and excitedly waited for their arrival. The one we wished most to see was Lord Ashley who we knew from reputation had tattooed hands, and that was enviable because it antedated our own period, which considered it incorrect, according to modern nautical ethics.

The Admiralty trooped down the quay and took their seats in the boat and I gave the orders: "Let go Bow" – "Back Starboard" – "Pull Port," and we swung off in the swiftly racing stream. While feeling out the boat I was suddenly horrified to find the rudder was unworkable.

Greenhithe was then a great yachting center, and the course between us and the *Worcester* was spotted generously by small boats laying at anchor. Before I had scarcely realized that I had no control over our boat, we struck one of these, scraped around its bow, its bowsprit sweeping off the hats of our distinguished guests. Never had the Admiralty of England, due to negligence, been submitted to such an insult. We scarcely cleared one yacht when we struck another, and then again we struck as we were helplessly swept by the stream. Clearing the third yacht I ran back over the grating, tore loose the useless tiller ropes and took the yoke in my hand. From then on it was comparatively plain sailing. Some darned boatmen, with a perverted sense of humor, had, when we were absent in the cook-shop, devoted the time to re-reeving the tiller ropes so that they nullified each other, and the slightest pull would lock the rudder. To a hurried glance the ropes would have shown no evidence of having been tampered with.

Once I had my hand on the rudder I had complete control but the damage had been done, and I was the most humiliated boy in the Empire, whose mortification had occurred before the eyes of every boy manning the yards. As we swung to make the gangway, and were yet a hundred yards from the ship, the chief officer on the upper deck, cupping his hands, yelled, "Captain of the Signals, what in the Hell are you doing?"

I could stand no more. Standing up on the grating I squeaked in a shrill treble, "Chief Officer of the *Worcester*, what in the Hell do you think?"

This was not so much an act of insubordination as it was an expression of utter despair. My pride was so wounded at my disgraceful showing, that no punishment could be a threat. What had I to fear? How could I be hurt anymore? It was impossible for anyone to hurt me more than I had hurt myself.

There was one ray of sunshine. As I looked along my oarsmen, calculating the landing I saw among the gloomy faces of the passengers one that was smiling. One human had found amusement in the mishap.

When I had the boat made fast I went on deck and was immediately ordered "between the guns." The punishment of "between the guns" was more a reproach, and the prelude of what would come after. You were expected to take your stand in the small space between two cannon and stay within that area, under the curious gaze of your fellows until summoned to the Captain's Court for trial and sentence.

When the Admiralty finished their inspection, another crew returned them to the shore, and I was summoned to the Captain's cabin. The Captain after listening to my story said justly, that I was responsible, because, while in charge of the boat, I had no right to leave it myself, or allow the crew to do so. Final sentence was suspended, but my liberty was stopped and I was ordered to stand in recreation hours for three days, between the guns. Whatever punishment I was to receive was a matter of indifference to me. I could be hurt no more, so I became sullen.

The second day I was again piped to lay aft and the Captain told me that I should keep my rank, but would be forbidden shore leave.

They used a system on the *Worcester* of transmitting orders through the seamanship instructors who shouted the text after giving a preliminary whistle on the pipe. Each instructor on the other decks would repeat the order and the pipe until the order was filled, or the boy sought found.

The third day I was again piped to the Captain's cabin. I saluted the sentry and stepped in, immediately behind the Captain's back as he sat at his desk. Without looking around he picked up a letter, scanned it awhile, and said, "Captain of the Signals, were you coxswain of the gig the day the Admiralty came on board?"

I did not know what the joke was, I had been on the mat before him twice already for that offense, so I answered, "You know darn well I was."

This hit his funny spot. I could see the back of his somewhat stout neck shaking as he laughed to himself. He took no notice of my impudent reply but continued, "I have a letter here from Mr. Clements Markham who was in the boat the day the Admiralty called, and he asks if the coxswain of the gig could be allowed to spend the next weekend with him." Then he turned in his chair and said, "Will you go?"

I was amazed. I came expecting some further punishment and here I was being rewarded. I could scarcely control my voice when I said, "I'll be glad to go!"

"Well," he said, "Leave is granted."

I procured the address and left the cabin in a dream. I had scarcely traveled half the deck length when a horrible thought occurred to me. I hadn't a penny. The last I had went for tarts. I returned to the captain's cabin and saluted. He looked around annoyed and said, "What do you want?"

I said, "I can't go."

He said, "Why?"

"I've no money."

He reached into his pocket, pulled out a pound and said, "Get out of here."

I got. It was no trouble for me to throw a few things in a bag and in an hour I was ashore and on my way to London. I did not know where I was going but it was away from the *Worcester*.

That evening I rang the bell at the address I had been given in Eccleston Square. The door was opened by a quietly dressed butler, and I was ushered into the study where my host sat at a desk. My host greeted me with a smile --- he was the possessor of the one smiling face in the boat on that fateful day the Admiralty called.

I had found a friend who for forty years kept a hospitable door open to me whenever I was in England, and when away, cheered me with friendly letters wherever I wandered.

Mr. Clements Markham was at that time President of the Royal Geographic Society, and was one of the greatest living travelers. The house was always a meeting place of men who had done something or been somewhere and it was a royal opportunity when the rudder stuck and I was precipitated into such a port of travelers.

His influence was of sufficient importance with the *Worcester* authorities to be able to get me the privilege of visiting him on weekends and at least once a month, he was kind enough to exercise this power.

4

Later Boyhood

At Hyde Hall conditions were altered from those of Mother's time. My Father's sister, Aunt Emma (which we abbreviated into "Temma") had taken charge of the household and she thought she had taken charge of the family, but as she was small, shy and timid, we bullied her shamelessly. She had lived to past middle age in a rural town with a sufficient income for her needs and now had been ruthlessly torn loose from her peace and quiet and was attempting to administer a rule in what to her was bedlam. Everything appalled her, the noise; the number of people; the butcher bills which in a month amounted to a year of her income; and yet a duty, and I know now, an affection, held her as administer of the family fortunes until father remarried.

We boys, probably due to less restraint became rowdier and our exuberance was let out through the sporting bent, of which dogs were generally the medium. In the neighbourhood were many large grain houses in which were caught during the month many rats and it was considered a pastime to watch a fight between a dog and a hundred rats in the cement grain pits, and we would gamble on the survivor – rats or dog. Then we considered dog fighting a sport and our private dogs had to have a reputation as fighters or they were a disgrace to possess.

We had another pastime which was by no means ladylike. We used to forage for cats, and when they were secured in a sack, we would take them into a meadow behind the house and course them. These meets were often attended by twenty dog owners with their dogs, and by familiarity we were able to handicap the dogs so that their speed over a given distance was nearly equalized. Each owner would put a shilling in the pool and then take his stand with his dog on the line which his handicap called for. Being thus all set, we shook the cat from the sack and the owner of the dog that first got the cat, pocketed the pool. We were not greedy for the pool, but we were proud if our dog distinguished himself. As the cat had one chance in twenty to get to the woods in the corner of the field, the supply became exhausted and although we foraged for miles trying to entice an unsuspecting tabby away from his back door, we seemed to have utilized the local supply. After two or three Saturdays without a meet, we decided to import the quarry. In England there was a journal called, "Exchange and Mart", which advertised to exchange everything from popguns to elephants. Through this channel we heard of a lady about to travel who wished a kind home for a family of cats. One of us wrote as we imagined a doting female would, whose life was lonely for the company of cats, and by return the cats arrived. Next Saturday we held a meet.

We might have gotten by with this piece of cruelty if someone hadn't persuaded us that it was funny, and once a week we would write the lady a bulletin of the joys those cats gave us as they played with our worsted and lapped cream while we knitted by the fire. Our humor became too raw, and instead of the usual letter an agent of the S.P.C.A made a visit. Father paid ten pounds and very fittingly we turned to more humane entertainments. The story sounds very heinous, but I doubt if it is. Every boy at this age is potentially cruel, and the healthier they are the more indifferent they act toward suffering. I am very positive that all those who were at these meets, when they eventually became conscious of what pain really meant were as softhearted and charitable as society will allow.

While recounting my misdeeds of this period I must mention my intolerance toward the servants. This was mostly in evidence with the grooms and gardeners, as fundamentally I was trained to be gentle to women which gave the house servants an immunity from persecution. The boot-boy, kennel-man and stablemen were all victims. This was more thoughtlessness than meanness, because with my lack of economic philosophy I had no way of deducing their dependence on my insolence. I unreasonably considered they were born that way, and I let it go at that.

I was always upsetting the order of the stable by feeding horses at the wrong time, or the wrong ration, pulling harness over, and otherwise showing a disagreeable energy in regulating affairs to suit my own sense of reform. The most open feud was between myself and Freeman, an old and very independent Scotchman, in charge of the greenhouses, which were extensive, running several hundred feet, and they raised hothouse grapes which were the pride of the county. I would walk through and pull a grape from occasional bunches. When I say that the grapes were not served if the bloom were even brushed, and Freeman wished every bunch intact, it is evident why friction existed. He would try to bribe me with an entire bunch, but with a perverse streak, I would pull single grapes until the storm commenced. It appeared to me that with such profusion one or a dozen bunches made no difference. How many Scotchmen make a passion of growing plants?

Freeman also raised tomatoes, which nowadays may sound commonplace, but then they were so rare as to be almost unknown. I remember Father would eat them raw and descant on this rare West Indian product and its value to the human system as a blood food.

My favorite companion was Cass, one of the under-gardeners of whom I was very fond. If I could not get him permission to accompany me I accompanied him as he did his work. He went with me shooting and rabbiting, and I helped him pot flowers and vegetables and replant flower beds. He was an elderly man with a large family which lived in a cottage close to the place. I would visit his home which I was told showed on my part a depravity of taste, but I saw for the first time that life was not easy to all, and although much was hidden from me, I sensed then, and now realize that Cass had a desperate struggle keeping those many craws full.

I was also a thorn in the flesh to my Father and often started discussions which he considered unorthodox. My subjects had a wide range and I was quick to detect the sore spot. Heretics, Atheists, housing the poor, Nihilism, Divine Right was part of the ammunition I used. He was an ordained minister and on occasions he took the pulpit in the village church, and from this vantage his eyes of necessity had to frequently rest on the front pew which we occupied. Here when his glance was sweeping toward us, I could gravely consult my watch, and after a long gaze, snap it shut with a click. I was nearly always rewarded by seeing him flinch, but the comedy was performed so gravely that he had no ground to reprove me without meeting a fairly plausible alibi.

The favorite humor in the family was ironic, and sarcasm was a vogue that obtained skill. At meals we were compelled to behave, but it was the occasion of unsheathing our more delicate weapons and the banter was always sharp, if not entertaining. There was but one restriction, -- vulgarity was impermissible. My Father's taunt and reply to my jibes was a request not to practice my "nautical humor" or my "For'castle wit in a gentleman's house."

On the *Worcester* time passed quickly. I was now in a position where I got many considerations in shore liberty. Occasionally I spent a few days with my Grandmother (Forbes) who had used most of a large fortune in suing the British government for the return of the Family estates which had been confiscated to the Crown in the Scotch rebellion of 1745. The only satisfaction she got was spending her money but she still remained very Scotch. If a chance wandering piper should happen into the street in a hope of English pennies, she would send out a maid to summon him (or them). She could sit for hours in a small room with the deafening scream of the bagpipes and be lost in the glories of the race she loved. She had become my closest feminine attachment. I admired and respected her austere character immensely, and our understanding was not broken until her death.

On one of these visits to my Grandmother I heard for the first time over a telephone. In Westminster Aquarium, a large glass amusement palace, the latest of the American inventions had been installed. At one end of the hall in a closed room a man played a cornet and on the other end of the building you sat at the receivers. For sixpence (12 cents) you were privileged to listen for a limited time and the experience was so novel we thought it was a most profitable way to spend twelve cents.

I went often to Mr. Markham's and always had a good time. It was not only a relief from the *Worcester* but it was a splendid chance for me to meet personalities I admired. He would give dinners to persons who had distinguished themselves in a certain field. There was an arctic dinner in which the food (including birds' eggs and dried ptarmigan) was imported from Norway and Greenland, and the guests (excepting myself) had with honor to themselves, been previously familiar with the peculiar food. Then there were dinners in which African hunters or Peruvian explorers were the principal guests, and I, a much dignified kid, was allowed to be present.

On the *Worcester* my name was mentioned about this time for an appointment as a midshipman in the Royal Navy, but Captain Smith suggested that the acceptance would be unwise. He certainly knew something of me and doubtless his affection told him that the discipline of the Navy would be too much of a test and something would be wrecked. As it was improbable I could wreck the Queen's Navy, the wreck would be myself, and he perhaps thought I should be spared so early in life such dangerous navigation.

The years moved fast and happily. I discovered another original method to make myself a nuisance to the masters on the *Worcester*. I had become so proficient in the routine studies that I could at will take a place near the top of the sixth form. This I would periodically do, and then with diabolical cunning begin to flunk examinations and slide in a few weeks to the third class from the bottom. Below that I was afraid to go without detection. I make this trip from top to bottom four times without suspicion of a deliberate design, and it was with huge glee that I then submitted to a mental test by a physician. Mr.

Urkhardt the master of the sixth form became so worried that he called for help. I had become a specimen for psychoanalysis, and he would take me on shore for walks with him alone, so that he could study the mental reactions which caused these relapses. On my part this was very unfair to him, because he was personally fond of me, but the pastime of kidding the whole school force was too fascinating to easily relinquish. I succeeded in my deceit, and told no one but Mr. Markham, and only him because I was bursting to make a confidant. Mr. Markham with a twinkle in his eye, professed to be shocked, and I promised him to work. The *Worcester* gave as school prizes some very valuable instruments including sextants, barometers and aneroids, which were mounted with silver shields inscribed with the name of the winner and the occasion. I asked him what he would think the most useful and said an aneroid. On looking over the list of prizes I saw an aneroid was to be given for first prize in navigation. At the end of the term Mr. Markham got his aneroid and it sat on his desk for the next forty years.

One of the swagger stunts on the *Worcester* was to swim the Thames which was about a mile across – and if you swum it one way you had to swim it twice to connect again with your clothes and ship. Before this sport was stopped by a boy nearly drowning and having to be rescued, those that determined to make it would go up a mile above the village, undress, hide their clothes and drop in. When they reached the Essex side they were, due to the tide a mile below or above the starting point. To counteract the current, you would have to walk the bank two miles in the direction the tide came from, before starting the home stretch. To have done this once entitled you to a niche in the school hall of fame. I made it once and knew I did not want to do it again.

Most of us wanted to be tattooed. The design on the old shellbacks who were our seamanship instructors, were to us too suggestive of the sea legends to not follow the example. We were our own designers and I imagine there are few of the boys of that period who do not carry a record of some schoolmate's artistic sense.

At Hyde Hall we changed our pastimes with the years. My eldest brother, being from his superior qualifications, a favorite with the elders, I always met him pugnaciously, and every so often I compelled him to lick me, but lived in hope and practiced boxing to aid my ambition. At least I was not picking on a weakling, as he was a splendid physical specimen, and all I got for my pains was the worst of it. The truth was I was jealous of everything he was.

One summer we spent in Wales and my second eldest brother and I, going swimming at the mouth of a river which was flowing out, were unconsciously swept to sea by the current. When we realized our predicament, land was nearly out of sight. Here for the first time I approached close to death, and was forced to admit my brother Charlie, was the better swimmer and had more confidence than myself. Due to his encouragement I got back to shore but I was nearly finished. The first boulder I could touch, I was grateful to tangle my fingers in its seaweed and let each incoming wave lift me up and drop me again on its encrusted barnacles. I was too far gone to protect myself and allowed my stomach and legs to be jagged in every descent. The suffering was cheap at the price. It was an important event in my life. For the first time I had become acquainted with real fear. This experience we kept to ourselves. The thought of being considered fools overbalanced any desire of sympathy.

The village church stood at the end and squarely in the centre of the main street and the clock in the tower was in sight of those on the street. One Saturday while walking through the churchyard to the village I noticed there was a tall ladder reaching half way to the clock with which the sexton was trimming the ivy. It occurred to me that with the aid of the ivy a boy could scale the clock. The next thought was that a leering face painted on the clock would have the effect of a surprise and shock to the village.

Taking my second eldest brother, Charlie, into the project, we secured some yellow paint and a brush from the tool house. We left the drawing room early that night, apparently to go to bed and once in our room we slid to the ground on a rope ladder I had constructed. There was nothing to prevent us from going downstairs and out through one of the doors, but this proceeding seemed hardly in keeping with such nefarious nocturnal work. Walking a mile to the church, we climbed the ivy and decorated the clock with a face. Dropping paint down the main street, and in the opposite direction to our home, we swung around, threw the paint pot in the canal and climbed the rope ladder to my bedroom window.

Next day, Sunday, we were on time for church, even a little early, and listened to the crowd to the indignant comments. The paint droppings had been discovered, the villains had left a clue and they would soon be discovered and arrested. The miscreants are still unpunished.

To raise money for what reason I know not, I sold all the books which had been given me as Christmas and birthday presents and as I had many, the proceeds were comparatively princely. I also sold my silver christening set; this netted me a larger return.

As boys we must have been a handsome bunch, but we were never allowed to become conscious of the fact. Our training was to minimize good looks as an achievement in itself. My brother Ernest, much resembled me, and I remember an uncle who amused himself by always reassuring the one that he was then alone with, that at least he could comfort himself he was not as ugly as the other. This was some comfort as long as we believed him and it was years before we compared notes. It was then too late to destroy the good he had done us. I was thirty-five years old before I would even allow myself to speculate whether or not I might be good looking.

Father since Mother's death, had changed much. He was quieter and more resigned and his amiability was less seldom ruffled. He was also getting stouter and took what he called exercise to reduce. This consisted in going with two of the men on the place into the woods with an intention of cutting wood. The two hired men would stand and brag on Father, and the accomplishment of the three amounted to less that the work of one, but they all got pleasure out of it, so the results were beneficial.

At the beginning of my fifteenth year, after 5 years on the *Worcester* training ship, which specialized in preparing officers for the sea, I was graduated and declared ready for active service. I was sorry to say goodbye to her, and all those in her who had treated me so well.

5

A Clipper Ship in 'Eighty

The Northumberland
historic photo

My Father, by paying 100 pounds, apprenticed me to the shipping firm of Shaw, Savill and Company, and I was assigned to their full rigged ship the *Northumberland* which was sailing in two months to New Zealand. My chum on the *Worcester*, Jack Callon, graduating at the same time, also made the same ship and so when I left England for the first time I would carry a friend with me.

The two months were given mainly to visiting. I remember I stayed a week with a relative who was minister in a model village on a model estate belonging to the Walter's, the hereditary owners of the London Times. I dined once at their home and ate for the first and last time off solid gold. The entire dessert service was of this metal which at the time impressed me as a significant exposition of refinement.

While there, I also went over the Huntley & Palmer Biscuit Factory, which was close by at Reading, and this I thought a great incident.

The outfit bought for my voyage included almost everything anyone suggested that could be useful for my comfort. Seaboots, oilskins, warm underclothes in abundance, with suits for shore and reading matter, which of course included a Bible. I was not to suffer from physical or moral exposure if provision could spare me.

As there was during the last week a little doubt of the exact date of sailing, I stayed at Mr. Markham's. Finally, the date was definitely given and we were ordered to report one afternoon and sail the next day. At Mr. Markham's suggestion, and after consulting the tides, it was decided to spare me the strangeness of the apprentice's quarters as long as possible. We determined I could make the ship at four in the morning and still be on time.

At 2 a.m. the house was aroused, and after breakfast, Mr. Markham bundling me into a cab, with my trunk on the roof, and accompanied me to the East India Docks where the *Northumberland* lay moored. It was a cold, damp morning, and the East end of London is at any time the most depressing district in the world to drive through. The squalor and the poverty, and the hour, had an effect on our spirits, and as we made our way to the ship, pushing through a medley of wives, prostitutes, crimps, drunken sailors, and dock riff-raff, we realized that sea-going had in it some elements which made none for romance.

Mr. Markham, while watching forty drunken and turbulent sailors being introduced by no gentle methods to the for'castle which was to be their home for a year, determined not to let me sail, but I felt that, having started it was up to me to see it through, and I resisted (with increasing shudders) his persuasion. With an affectionate farewell, I saw him on his way back to his cab and civilization.

We were carrying to New Zealand, four hundred passengers for whom accommodations were made between decks, but before our arrival these had been herded below and the hatches closed and I was unaware of their existence.

Working with dockmen and those of the crew who were not too drunk to be of service, the ship was warped through the dock gates, where a tug, making fast a towline, we were swung into the main channel of the Thames and headed toward to the sea. I was stunned and dizzy with this startling change in my life and felt sick to my soles with disgust. I had never before been in contact with drunkenness and this first experience so full of degrading details shocked every sense I possessed. I mooned around disconsolately for an hour, avoiding contact or duty until the novelty of the passage brought some renewed interest.

No one seemed interested in me and I was given no duties. I searched for and found Jack Callon, who was sitting disconsolately in his bunk. We tried to cheer each other without effect.

In an hour we were summoned to breakfast in the apprentices' mess and we met the other five boys who were to be our companions, but at the time they made no impression on me. I wanted to forget. The meal suggested the drunken state of the crew and was untouched. In two hours we were at Gravesend after passing the *Worcester*, which got a forlorn stare from Callon and myself. For some reason (probably to complete clearance papers) we moored to a buoy at Gravesend and the tug left us. At noon I was lolling around the deck watching the shipping, and wondering if I dare tackle the dinner when I saw a boat from the shore approaching the ship. When it made the gangway its passenger climbed on deck and it was Mr. Markham. Hearing by telegraph that the ship would be held a few hours he had come down to renew his persuasion that I abandon the trip. He offered to provide for my future in any other manner I saw fit, but I had now definitely made up my mind that however disagreeable I would make the voyage, and Mr. Markham returned to shore leaving behind a memory that has sweetened my life.

Toward evening the tug again hooked to us and we swung down the river with the tide. The hatches had been removed to give the passengers air and some of them came up to breathe. The decks were still disorderly with the cursing and quarrelling crew which drove the women and children back to their stuffy quarters. The men appeared a wholesome type of the best English farmers who hoped for cheaper land and better conditions in New Zealand. To take my mind from my unhappy state I assisted in every duty I could be useful in, and won the lasting goodwill of the second mate who was nearly distracted with his difficulties.

Night came. We seemed to be rushing past the shore lights, each looking like a lost friend as it dropped astern and disappeared. At two in the morning we were in the open Channel and the tug cast us loose. The mainsails and topsails were set in a great confusion of orders. The second and third mates had to actually lead the men aloft to be sure the work was fittingly accomplished. The second mate showed some dependence on my assistance and I was forgetting my woe in the pleasure of being recognized as a useful unit. As the ship moved under her own way I was part of the force which governed the whole. If I wished to be a sailorman, leaving port was part of the game and not to be dwelt on. I was at sea.

More sail was slowly shaken loose and set. The first and second mates then mustered the crew and picked their watches, taking an alternate choice until all had been assigned. After the first few selections which covered those sober I don't know what reasoning they used. Perhaps a second sight comes with experience, which tells how much of a sailorman a drunk is when sober, or maybe the dim light of the lantern made the choice only a matter of guess anyway. The second mate picked me the first when dividing the apprentices and won my loyalty thereby. I felt more than a cipher. I was an individual. Our watch was set below and having been on my feet nearly twenty-four hours, I wasted little time in unrolling my bedding, throwing it in a bunk and crawling in somewhere in the middle. In four hours we would be called, and for the next three months we would never get more than that time between watches on deck.

With light winds for twelve hours, we were headed west under full sail, then there was a change, the wind shifting to the southwest and freshening into a gale. Slowly as we beat in the face of the storm, the sail was, one by one, reduced to topsails, mainsails and a jib. The passengers who had been allowed on deck during the day were again sent below, due to the hurry in operating the ship, and the water coming on board from the choppy sea. Before night the wind had increased, and the upper topsails were close reefed. For five days we beat against a heavy storm without making an inch of headway. We ceaselessly tacked across the channel, the ship being put about every two hours, and always we saw the same landmarks. By day the town, by night the lights of Hastings in England or Boulogne in France, greeted us on the end of each tack in exactly the same position.

If I had been looking for experience in seafaring it would have been difficult to get any quicker action. Every two hours all hands were needed to "bout ship". Two or three times her nose hung in the wind and the alternate and more difficult tactic of "ware ship" had to be undertaken on a lee coast. It was bitterly cold, the decks awash. Oilskins and seaboots were scarcely shed when they had to be again donned, and sleep and food were a secondary consideration to be snatched in the lulls of work. The passengers were not only driven below, the hatches were put on and the tarpaulins battened over them to keep the water out of the hold. Why the Captain did not put back into port I don't know. But these were the days of clipper ships and putting back in port was not a habit encouraged. Perhaps he legitimately considered the storm would slacken or vary, instead of holding us for five days in an iron grip.

Here I got my first rum ration. The crew were too frazzled with work and shore dissipation to stand up to the work without it, and every watch of the storm each man got a third of a glass of raw spirit. I never missed stepping in line and was grateful of the thrill as it raced through my blood to my cold extremities.

To make our position more tantalizing there was always passing sailing ships homeward bound. They were scudding before the gale to the port we had left, or to the North Sea, and steamboats, close enough to suggest the comforts we were lacking, would pass us going in both directions, making an easy way in comparison with ourselves.

Below everything was confusing to a novice. The *Northumberland* although iron and modern, was laboring like she suffered from internal cramps, and the partitions and bulkheads kept up a constant squeaking and groaning. For some reason I escaped seasickness. Callon was completely incapacitated in the bunk above mine.

The only humor I found in the five days was during the second night while snatching a sleep in my watch below. We had no light; the night was full of strange noises; and the ship was lurching and rolling in a way that suggested to a novice she couldn't survive. I had also seen and recognized the difficulties with the crew, and the dangers of being beached. I went to bed nursing the conviction that I was too young to die, and, given another chance, I would try to live a better life. I fell asleep in this mood and drifted into a nightmare from which I awoke to find myself tightly pressed by a heavy and solid weight, and while not knowing exactly what had happened, I knew the end was at hand. I lay in terror; I saw no hope in crying out, and I could not move; and then, I heard a moan close to me. What was this? I did not know, but apparently I was not to die alone. Then I heard, "I wish I was dead." Such a sentence should bring joy to none, but it did to me. It was a phrase I had heard Callon sighing for the last two days. The weight holding me down was Callon and not the wreck of the ship. The working of the hull had loosened his bunk boards on the outside of his bunk and in falling like a hinge with his bedding, he had pinned me up against the ship's side in a suffocating crack. If you want to see a bully get into action to advantage give him a good scare first. When I realized there was no danger I cussed Callon. Too sick for resentment, he lay where he had fallen and I made him get up and help me fix the bunk, and I'm sure I was not silent as we blundered around in the dark. I felt at the time that it was an outrage that a non-worker such as he, should disturb the peaceful and necessary sleep of one upon whom so much depended as myself.

Everything has an end; we weathered the storm and rolled under full sail toward the Atlantic. Hatches were removed, sleep gathered, and with passengers lolling and children playing on deck, all seemed to have forgotten that we had lately been skirting the threshold of disaster. With the sunshine, -- the wind and the sea as if ashamed of its past display of temper showed nothing but their amiable qualities. With the change of condition, the order for which the sailormen have a talent began to be demonstrated, and the discipline of a smart ship wiped away the traces of land.

The apprentices lived in separate quarters from the crew, but I had several times been in the forecastle to help the officers man the watch.

This contact with drunken and maudlin men wallowing in the filth of a debauch had been to me a horrid experience. All this was changed. The sailors were voluntarily washing themselves and their quarters, and order was being established among themselves. In a big ship of the old days, there was a pride of efficiency among sailormen and a recognition of such mastery among themselves. This status was now being established among the forty-two men before the mast and there were several battles of bulls before the matter was decided finally. I remember one royal fight between a big American and a Finlander. Leadership had various prerogatives and one was to hold the hose and direct the stream in washing the decks while the others used the brooms. These two quarreled over the hose privilege and as they were both physically fine specimens it took twenty minutes of savage fighting to decide the seniority. The American won, and I must say that once the victor established his superiority it was accepted, and not questioned for the rest of the voyage.

I had one unpleasant experience in connection with the crew which might have had serious consequences. One of the sailors named Carney, had been hit on the head with a bottle from which erysipelas started. It was my duty to help move him to a separate cabin and partially care for him. I thought him completely unconscious when someone asking me if he were dead, and I flippantly replied, "No, but he should be."

He heard me and broke out into a torrent of the vilest billingsgate. I felt sorry that I had made the remark but he never forgave me. Nearly eight months later while aloft at night in a storm off the Horn, I felt a pressure from the next oilskin-clad figure. When aloft, both hands may be engaged or only one, but always the sailor makes only provision for safety from his own carelessness; the acts of others are not being taken into consideration. In this case I thought at first the jostling had been accidental, but slowly I knew it to be intentional. Then, after a protest I recognized Carney. The old hound by bearing his weight on me was deliberately trying to force my chilled hands loose, and let me drop in the sea which on such a night would be unnoticed. He had probably been watching for this opportunity and followed me aloft thinking the conditions suitable. I never mentioned the incident except to Callon.

The home sickness had left me entirely. I was now intent on nothing more than becoming a good sailor and cheerfully volunteered for any duty the second mate considered desirable. The boys of a ship had complete control of the handling of the lighter canvas on the highest yards and these were furled and unfurled on slight changes in the wind, which to a landsman were imperceptible. The lightest puff was taken advantage of, and a captain's reputation was made by his mileage. Many clippers left port about the same time, encountering nearly similar weather conditions and the rivalry between the Captains and ships was intense, the crews sharing the feeling.

Everybody appeared contented. The passengers reveled in a sunshine unknown to the landbound Englishman, and were happy that they were headed toward a land of promise. To Callon and myself their presence on the ship was a godsend. We made friends with many of them and softened the rigor of our new life. In perfect weather we sailed by the Island of Tenerife and in the shadow of its great mountain. This was the first and last land we were to see until our arrival one hundred days later in Auckland.

After a few days of breathless calm in the tropics, we crossed the equator to the southern hemisphere and there was the usual play in initiating those who had not before crossed the line. The occasion was made a festive one by the 400 passengers, much of the rawness being modified to keep from giving them offense, and on this account we escaped being shaved with a barrel hoop with tar used for soap, and other strenuous illustrations of nautical humor which were ordinarily considered appropriate. The penalty enacted was a ducking in a large canvas tank, but the fun was universal and nothing occurred to make the day anything but a holiday.

Keeping no track of the days we rounded the Cape of Good Hope without sighting land and ran into the Easting. The "Easting" is that strip of water between the Cape and Australia, and here the packets bound to the Colonies made their time. The wind in this quarter is almost continually from the west and comes as a stiff breeze that often rises to a gale. For weeks we clipped along making better time than the then existing steamships and our daily run was from 220 to 285 knots.

It is an exhilarating experience to be one time on a full rigged ship running before a stiff breeze, and feel the tension which comes to her hull when a fresher gust lifts her under your feet to greater effort. To watch the great white sails spread against the blue sky catching and utilizing every breath; and then look sternward at the giant rollers forever trying to catch the ship, and failing, fall a tumbling cascade as if in petulance. Not a whisper of wind but what an effort was made to take advantage of it, trimming the yards to spill nothing. The officer of the watch stood heedful for any variations in the puffs, his eyes strained to the smaller and most vulnerable canvas. I have climbed to the highest yard and set a sail twice in one watch and furled it as often. Manpower was plentiful—what they wanted was miles. No spars were broken on this trip but three times sails were blown away, only for new ones to be immediately bent and shaken out in the first lull. Thus they sailed when competing with steam and the name of many of the sails we apprentices handled are now no longer in the nautical vocabulary. Slow going steamboats would be cited ahead, overhauled and left astern, unable to contend with us.

The apprentices had the privilege of the after deck, and in my watches off duty I caught several albatross, one measuring twenty feet from tip to tip of wing. These beautiful birds have a hooked bill and with a piece of pork tied on a triangle of steel they fell an easy victim. They would snap at the pork and the moment they felt the steel they obstinately set their web feet to pull against the line and this with the speed of the ship set the steel firmly in the hook of their upper bill. The pulling them aboard was only a matter of labor. I cleaned and preserved three breasts which were a heavy white down fully two inches thick, checked three inches apart by one coal black feather, the whole making a beautiful mat nearly two-foot square.

The birds pick up a ship at the Cape and follow it for forty days or two months until close to Australia and they seemed indifferent to speed. Every morning by their individual marking you recognized the same birds. When they slept has always been a mystery to me. Arriving near port they deserted to return with another ship to the Cape.

A little more than three months from England we made the port of Auckland and moored to the docks. Our passengers left us and the matter of discharging the cargo was at once undertaken. With the actual labor the apprentices were not asked to assist and our duties were only nominal. We had many letters of introduction, and intended to use them, but Callon and I, or rather I and Callon, decided that when we got on our first leave we would have a good time. We had money, and the first desire was a big feed with drinks included, then to a vaudeville show. After this we felt we had not acted as sailormen should and we went to a supper with more drinks. I soon became tipsy and boisterous, and to Callon's disgust refused to return to the ship with him as that appeared a tame ending to a first night ashore. His persuasion failing to move me he left alone and I continued what I thought was a good time. I went to bed with a chance acquaintance but awoke still fuzzy, in time to report on board at 6 a.m. I was sick, but also unexpectedly ashamed and disgusted with myself. This sense of humiliation made the experience appear a cheapening one, and I determined to abandon the career of a sport. Callon aided me in arriving at this conclusion by taking my defection personally, and we relied on finding other pleasure through the letters we carried.

One of these letters was to Sir George Grey, then Governor General of New Zealand. I favored presenting this letter because Sir George had an island off the coast stocked with many forms of wild game, but for the economy of time, we selected at random another letter for a resident of Auckland. In those days if you presented one letter, you never would find time to deliver any others you held. Never were there a more hospitable people and Callon and I were swept from one entertainment to another. I scarcely found time for my first calf love which was directed toward a charming girl, some ten years older than myself. She was a splendid tennis player, which counted for many points in selecting a life partner. My regard increased on the lonely voyage home and I wrote her a proposal to which she, to my surprise, replied with a suggestion that possibly a boy not yet sixteen should wait a few years before a final decision. I've forgotten her name.

From Auckland we went south to the Bay of Napier. The *Northumberland* was equipped as a refrigerator ship and constituted the first trial in shipping frozen meat from New Zealand to England. At Napier we were to load sixteen thousand mutton for the English market and while loading these we had another spell of entertainment ashore.

The Captain decided to try an experiment with oysters which were plentiful in the bay and hired Maori's to fish them for him. This was my first acquaintance with the New Zealand Maori and I was much fascinated by their wonderful physical perfection. Twenty of them, including both sexes, would paddle a big canoe (dug from a solid Karri tree) to the centre of the bay; and then completely nude commence diving for the oysters. Both men and women did the diving and I thought in the grace of their action and poise they formed a silent reproach to the more civilized races.

Fortunately for us on the *Northumberland* the oyster would not keep on ice, and as the government protected the natives, the contract had to be fulfilled. For weeks the Maoris dumped oysters on board and all we had to do for a feed was to get an iron belaying pin. We, at the Captain's expense, cracked oysters by the hour, and with the sea biscuit they made a pleasant change in the ship's diet.

Because of my interest in the Maoris, I determined to see some of their villages and there being a large one some sixteen miles inland, I hired a saddle horse to make the trip. On the way up the mountain I met long cavalcades of Maoris riding to the coast, and I learnt that on this day a benevolent government donated two blankets and a sack of flour to every adult male Maori who made application for the same. At the time I did not see the significance of this coincidence, but on the arrival at the village it appeared to be completely deserted. After inspecting several thatched dwelling houses with the cooking pottery, I found a more ambitious building which suggested either a place of worship or a counsel house. Its interior walls and exterior fences were decorated with curious and well-made carvings representing their deities and I became so interested that the time slipped away fast. Realizing I had to get back to the ship I started to my horse but was intercepted by several women who made signs which my modesty forbade me to interpret. As I tried to get to my horse the signs became demonstrations and I saw that as a preacher's son, I was in danger. The women enjoyed their sport and screamed with laughter at my embarrassment. With considerable scrambling, and at the price of a torn coat I got on my horse, but as I rode to the coast I knew that if I made further investigations I should select a day on which the native ladies could rely on the support of their legitimate protectors.

The New Zealand waters and particularly Napier Bay were bountifully supplied with fish, and we had fun keeping the crew in fresh food. Some varieties weighed fifteen to twenty pounds and I was smitten with the (then novel) idea to take frozen fish home to England. This scheme was never fulfilled. I caught and cleaned some half dozen and placed them in the frame of a frozen sheep, but from the excitement of our arrival in London, I forgot my fish and some deck laborer had the experience I intended as a surprise for my people.

In catching the fish every second one was a shark, and these gave a subject for an illustration of the deep-seated cruelty in humans when their fundamental fears and prejudices are aroused. The sailors, otherwise amiable men, would take these shark and torture them in every manner they could conceive, and even used the steam jet from the refrigerator plant. This blind hatred I could not then understand, nor can I do so now. There was here no way you could use the name of sport to mitigate the offense.

We had been laying in the harbor loading the mutton from lighters and when the cargo was complete we weighed anchor and sailed for home. The homeward passage was to be made without passengers and the space was devoted to freight.

When I said goodbye to New Zealand, I scarcely knew how many pleasant memories I would retain of it. My mind lingers on Auckland with affection, as the most desirable place of my travels. The wonderful climate, the hospitable people; the beautiful mountains and valleys stretching for miles behind the town; the big gum timber, the smells, the absence of poverty, all suggested the ideal land. Why did I not stay there? Why is it I never went back? It must be due to an abnormality in myself. I had many inducements—eager friends willing to welcome me, funds to invest in a profitable industry, energy and health; yet the years have passed and still finds me listening to the sound of the bells from over the hill. Reason assured me a peaceful and comfortable existence immune from trial and hardship. I would not listen then- I refuse to listen now. When Reason and I argue on my welfare, Reason is unfairly handicapped, and can seldom hope for a decision in its favor. I am not even sorry for my obstinacy—I am glad. I was called elsewhere to harder schools of life. Auckland to me was a dreamland—and for me only to be treated as a dream.

And the *Northumberland* was booming under full sail toward the Horn, which is no place to nurse dreams of salubrious climates; so let us be sailor men and work our ship home to London.

Readers of sea stories gain an impression that the sailor's life is a series of stirring events when it is in truth a very monotonous existence, particularly in the slower moving ships devoted to freight. The high spots of danger, if there are any, are separated by long periods of the most ordinary routine, and many voyages will be made without a sign of a thrill to the crew. After years at sea, a passing ship may have been the most exciting event recorded in the lives of many sailormen.

As the weeks passed on the *Northumberland*, we made our way across the Pacific, and a drenching in an unexpected rainstorm was a welcome variation to the order with which every situation was met and controlled. Calms, breezes, gales, squalls, fair winds, head winds, came and went, with only a temporary flurry of change. Sails were taken in, or shaken out, duties fulfilled, the ship steered, but all appeared as only a break, and something apart from the abiding sense of loneliness. The oceans are a vast thoroughfare, but outside of those beaten channels between large ports you may sail for a month without sighting a fellow wayfarer. In fair weather, which predominates, you scan the slightly rolling surface of the sea, and wonder what of the rest of the world. In our seven months' sailing and once we were clear of the port of departure or destination, we only came into close proximity with two other ships, and these at a distance of more than a mile. At times we saw ships on a far and tantalizing horizon, and endeavored to kill boredom by guessing at their port and nationality, but the certainty of our isolation would soon return and sink down on us like a pall.

I found my only redemption was work and I hunted it. Thus passed the hours on watch. The hours below were mostly filled by sleep, which an active boy can always use, with a little reading, from the bible, often because of no other choice. These were the days before phonographs and radios were known.

It was winter in the southern hemisphere, and as we neared the Horn it became bitterly cold. I remember one night I spent four hours aloft because I was so cold I dare not come down. To the uninitiated there is in a ship's rigging two points where the sailor to ascend or descend is nearly horizontal, as a fly on the ceiling. There was a cold sleet and I had been sent aloft to furl one of the higher sails. When this was finished I had so little power in my hands I was afraid to trust my weight to their grip. I managed to get to the crosstrees where there was solid footing, and then locking my arms around a wire stay, I thrust my hands into my oilskin under my armpits. When the circulation started a sense of feeling I could by hooking my elbows around the shrouds descend further, and by this method and in a number of trials I finally reached the deck. Fortunately, I hit a rum ration which had been reinstituted.

The weather was getting more threatening. The lighter sails were unbent and the upper yards sent down and lashed on the deck. Everything but the bare masts above the topgallant yards was stripped as we prepared for that terror of the sailorman—the passage of the Horn.

When due south of the Horn, the storm and sea increased tremendously. This gale from the west brought mountain rollers probably half a mile apart and so high that it appeared that no small shell like a ship could ride them in safety. Science has declared that no wave was ever over forty feet in height. To a sailorman, who, with his ship in the trough of two waves, has seen in a tearing gale the canvas fifty feet above the deck, flap idly against the mast for lack of air to fill them, and then as the vessel rose on the swell of one of these mountains of water, fill with a noise as the explosion of cannon the question arises as to where the statistics were gathered.

We were running dead (straight) before the gale and hitting the waves at right angles, or rather they were hitting us; because with the shortened sails our speed was so diminished that the waves caught up and curled over us. The sail was cut to three lower topsails, two close reefed upper topsails, and one jib, which cracked constantly with loud reports as it alternately filled and spilt on either side.

With the blow of the wave on the stern of the ship the steering was difficult, taking four persons to hold the wheel from being torn from their hands as the water struck the rudder with a weight of tons. Two men, with two boys on the lee side were assigned this duty, each for his protection having a rope from his waist to a ringbolt in the deck.

As you rode up the slope of the coming waves, with the swift rushing water you appeared to be slipping backward, until when near the summit the curl of the wave submerged you, and the ship was buried beneath the water. Everybody on deck wore a rope and watched that he was not caught unprepared. As the ship struggled back to the surface you felt the ship's hull tremble and quiver under your feet as she threw off the weight of water that covered her.

The watch at the wheel was one hour in which time you nearly froze, and one night after I was relieved I was picked up by the water and it seemed, rushed for miles to sea. Seconds appearing eternal, I thought I was beyond hope when I truck an iron rail. If ever a boy clung to salvation that rail should bear witness. The sea passed and I found myself hung to the rail of the for'castle ladder. I was a grateful youth, but how I had traveled but that short distance of forty feet in the incredible space of time—I had thought I was being carried to sea – is to me still a mystery.

The jib's mission was to keep the ship's nose before the wind, and when it once blew away there was nearly two hours dangerous and freezing labor bending a new one, while the ship broadside to the sea, rolled fearfully; the masts threatening to snap themselves with the jerking strain.

With sail reduced to a minimum, barring accidents, the only work was steering, and everybody was allowed below except the officer of the watch and the helmsman. Here again a grog ration was a necessity. I was amply supplied with clothes of the most suitable kind and was able to change to dry ones, but hard as it may be to believe, many men before the mast endured this exposure with inferior seaboots and no change of suits. It is a wonderful tribute to the seafarer when you know that among forty men on the darkest night when shirking would be impossible of detection, you were certain every man pulled his pound regardless of his personal misery.

Captain Forbes was a man of whom nobody on board with the exception of the officers knew much. He was a small man with a complexion which suggested drink, though he never showed any indications of its use, and whenever seen on deck, he was dressed with a white collar and tie, as if for shore. There was a rumor, probably started by the steward that for his consumption three quarts of spirits went into his cabin each day; a bottle of whiskey in the morning, rum at noon and brandy at night. Also, the cabin, and his home on shore, was reported to be stocked with silver plates given him by owners grateful for the quick passage of his commands. All of this may have been purely for'castle gossip. If the steward had said it, he did not make a habit of repeating it and only he knew. The Captain had never been heard to give an order or speak to any of the crew. If he had an order to give it was either given to the officers below, or if on deck, passed in quiet undertone. There was not a sign of the "Bucko" in him. The crew was practically unacquainted with him, as he, except on extraordinary occasions, only came on deck to make his observations of the sun at noon. When this was done, with a few muttered words to the mate in charge, a glance aloft and over the horizon, he went again below.

One night two of the topsails blew out, and the ship broached broadside and helpless on the sea. I happened to be helping on the wheel which was directly over the companionway to the cabin. The ship had scarcely given her first lurch when a figure in pajamas and bedroom slippers threw open the hatch and stood revealed as the Captain —come on deck to take command. If we had never before heard him give a direct command it was not because he was incapable. Yelling to make his voice heard above the wind, he directed the sailors to get up the new sails and bend them; the second mate leading the men aloft as an example. As order slowly evolved the Captain came aft and paced the deck directly before the binnacle watching the wind and sea and encouraging labor aloft. His slippers had washed away and the steward had brought him an oilskin and seaboots but his suffering from cold must have been intense. In less than three hours the sails were re-bent and set. The ship again in control, payed away before the wind and the Captain went below, not to noticeably take command of his own ship on the voyage. He had established himself as one of my heroes. Once a sailorman always a sailorman; and Captain Forbes was a sailorman.

I have never regretted my experience around the Horn. It left many memories I am glad of. When forty men, in the flooded waist of a ship, with decks awash and suffering from bitter cold, can respond to the discipline and overcome such incredible handicaps and physical misery, it must remain an inspiration.

We had a great chanty man with a splendidly deep and resonant voice and the picture arises in my mind of that voice coming from somewhere out of the dark, singing above the whistling wind:

"I thought I heard --- The Old Man say,
'WHISKEY----------JOHNNIE'
I thought I heard --- The Old Man say,
'WHISKEY --- for – MY – JOHNNIE.' "

The crew added their voices in rhythmic harmony at each "Whiskey" and "Johnnie", the words being the signal for forty backs to drag in unison at a frozen halyard; and aloft there was a responding squeak of blocks as the spar arose to its appointed place. Once heard, the certainty comes to you that there can be romance under nearly every condition if you look for it.

Slowly we were winning our way. Running before the wind we met beating against it, a full rigged ship, down to close reefed topsails. If we were miserable, here was a worse condition. This ship might have to battle for weeks before it made the Pacific. We passed her close, she scarcely moving. The seas were so high that we would lose sight of her between the waves, then see her again as we both rose to a crest again. She looked like a solid sheet of ice, every rope, spar and sail being covered, and as she nosed into the head sea, she appeared to sink under each wave that struck her to rise again and struggle forward a few more feet. We left her behind, but contemplating her difficulties made our own easier.

One other night, we hove to again. The second mate told me the Captain "felt ice" and had given the order. At daylight he was proven correct. We were in a field of broken ice floes. In that extreme cold the Captain had been warned by a fall in the temperature so imperceptible, others had not noticed it. With day the ice was easily avoided and in another twenty-four hours we were turning our nose each watch a little more to the North. The Horn was weathered, and we were headed to the tropics and warmth. To be dry and warm once more was the extreme of our desire.

Now the long passage of the Atlantic -- dreary uneventful weeks. We may have had a storm, but they did not record; we had seen storms. Rain or sunshine, what we wanted was home, all else was a means to an end and dismissed as such. A school of whale or porpoise, flying fish or dolphin, only meant a temporary break in the tiresome vision of the eternal emptiness of the surrounding water. The ship, dirty with seaweed and barnacles was making slow sailing and in the terrific heat of the tropics the refrigerator plant began to show incapacity. Firing with coal the firemen had all succumbed to heat and for desire of experience I volunteered. Working two-hour shifts, I lasted five days before I had enough and was relieved, but we were now in a more temperate zone and the situation was saved.

Eventually word was passed that with the prevailing wind we would make the English Channel next day. Again we were going into a winter; three winters in twelve months. We left England in the winter, struck winter in the southern hemisphere and returned to be again greeted with cold.

Before we sighted land a small dingy was seen dancing on the rough sea. The course of the ship was changed to go close to this tiny boat and it proved to be what was expected – a pilot. The pilot, a hearty good-natured giant in oilskins, came on deck, and was immediately served coffee. His companion was thrown a line and the boat dropped astern to be towed until we saw land next day. Within sight of England the line was cast off and the dingy made its way back to shore. For a sheltered people's understanding, it might not be amiss to recount what a man in 1880 expected to do for twenty-five dollars. To become a pilot a man had to have been a master of a ship and have passed a stiff Board of Trade examination to show his familiarity with the English Channel and the Thames River. Then for employment he must establish a home at Land's End, Cornwall; obtain a dingy and hire a boatman. To get his existence he must connect with ships, and for this he put to sea and intercepted a homeward-bound packet which picked him up. In all weathers, he with his companion at the chance of their lives, spent days in an open boat waiting an opportunity to earn a living. A ship secured, the pilot took her to London, was discharged, paid his own fare back to Cornwall, connected with his boatman and pushed off again to the open sea to find another ship. And for these five, six, eight, or ten-day jobs, he received a five-pound note.

Once in the Channel and in sight of land, events moved quickly. At the mouth of the river we picked up a waiting tug and the sails were furled and snugged down for the last time. As we raced up the river all was excitement. We passed our old training ship, the *Worcester*, and made the docks of London in time to clear the Custom House before night and sleep again in a bed ashore.

On our homeward passage we had sailed 144 days without sighting land. On the voyage we had circled the globe. With the exception of

Callon, the second mate was the strongest personal tie of affection the ship held for me. To him I said goodbye, little dreaming he was fated to fall from aloft on the next voyage and be lost. He was a real man and a sailor, and I had much to be grateful to him for. The street lights, the new faces, the noise of traffic, the very brick warehouses, all appeared a new and strange world and we were eager to be away to adventures untried.

6

On Sir Clements Markham

In Sir Clements Markham...

I had found a friend, one who for forty years kept a hospitable door open to me whenever I was in England and when away he cheered me with friendly letters wherever I wandered.

Gradually I learned that Mr. Markham, later Sir Clements Markham, was a famous explorer, traveler and author. At that time he was honorary secretary of the Royal Geographic Society, a post he filled for twenty-five years; five years later he was elected president of the Society which honor he held for twelve years. Certainly the success of the National Antarctic Expedition was largely due to Sir Clements' efforts which earned him the title of "Father of the Expedition." The choice of Captain Robert F. Scott as head of the Expedition was Markham's wish and the results of the Expedition proved it was a wise one.

After returning from the Arctic Expedition of 1850, Sir Clements began to explore Peru and the unknown forest of the Eastern Andes. He became interested in the cultivation of the cinchona or quinine trees. On his return to England he was appointed a member of the Board of Control which then governed India. He immediately pressed the importance of introducing the quinine trees into India for the purpose of reducing the price of quinine to allow the natives to purchase the drug in the malarious districts.

In 1860 he went to South America and successfully brought the trees to India. As a result of his splendid work the price of quinine dropped from ten shillings an ounce to one shilling in Calcutta. It is doubtful whether any single man has conferred a greater benefit on humanity than Sir Clements Markham did when he undertook to place quinine within reach of those who needed it sorely.

Sir Clements' home was always a meeting place for men who had done something eminently worthwhile. It was a royal opportunity when the rudder stuck and I was precipitated into such a port of travelers.

Since Sir Clements' death the strength of that friendship has often made me marvel. Even the fact that I joined the Boer forces in South Africa in 1899 and fought against my own country and the country which he had served with such distinction left the friendship unimpaired.

I have known good and bad, sin and virtue, right and wrong; I have judged and been judged; I have gone through death, joy and pain, heaven and hell; and what I realized in the end is that I am in all and all is in me.

~Hazrat Inayat Khan

II

Stories & Reflections

7

Bicoachi (Mexico)

We were fortunate in securing a large six room adobe house with a wide porch passing the plaza. This was the most important building in the village and belonged to the Alcalde. The rooms were spacious, and in the rear there was nearly an acre corral fenced with a six-foot adobe wall giving us accommodations for our stock. There were no modern conveniences in the way of plumbing and the water was brought daily in panniers or canvas sacks from the river by burros. When I started such a revolutionary innovation as building an outside toilet in the corral the entire population sat on the wall and jeered. They resented this implied Gringo reflection on their established habits of life.

Sunday evening the band played in the centre of the large plaza and the eligible marriage material walked like a school procession around the borders but the males and females seldom intermingled. The males promenading left to right and the females the reverse -- each watching for their particular imorata and giggling at each meeting.

We secured an excellent Chinese cook who was very responsible in our absence. On the subject of this cook I had a point of morals to adjust. Constantly other Chinamen warned us that he was crooked--- none of them would speak a good word for him. He was evidently an outcast among his kind. I decided that his service was the best obtainable and the percentage he could filch on the purchase of supplies, or in bulk was infinitesimal, so I took the chance and kept him. Of course, he knew that I had been warned and my unexpected action in retaining him won his gratitude, and a more faithful retainer could not have been desired, besides which he had a high order of intelligence for which I was the gainer by his companionship.

The hotelkeeper was our labor agent. I could speak a little Mexican and understood much more, but for reasons of my own I pretended complete ignorance of the language. This gave me many advantages in a country of which the population were admittedly hostile. To illustrate—I went into the hotel one day on business and the proprietor was playing cards in the back of the room. He gave a gesture or impatience, said to his companions, in Spanish—"Wait a minute until I see what the damned Chinaman wants" Then advance toward me greasily rubbing his hands he said in English---"How do you do, Senor Captain, What can I do for you today?"

Another local influence on the natives was my possession of an automatic Leuger pistol, a weapon then little known in America. As is known, it loads with a magazine in the handle and I always carried a dozen extra magazines in my pocket and had no visible shell belt. When I attended the shoots (public), I would shoot at the target with what to them was extraoardinary speed and precision. I never let them see me insert another magazine but palmed them into place. Thus sometimes I shot four, sometimes eight shots at one time. In all shooting 30-40 shots and for all they knew all the shells were in the gun form the beginning. This mystery always filled them with fear and fortunately for me--- respect.

Another reason why I was able to operate in this territory was due to a dog. Some six months previously while in Arizona a nondescript mongrel covered with red wool had come into camp one night when to the best of our knowledge there was not a settlement or camp within 30 miles. His hunger was evident and we fed him. He wished himself on us and appointed me his guardian so I named him "Ben" and from then on, he was my constant companion. As he was a tenderfoot and needed care; following my footsteps in the day he would walk blindly upon cactus limbs then try to pull them with his teeth with the result of filling both his jaws, tongue and feet with stickers, which I had to extract individually when camp was made for the night. Having constituted himself my bodyguard, I took his assumption seriously and by whatever method I travelled between our prospects he accompanied me to the disgust of stagedrivers and baggage men who bled me shamelessly because they considered me too weak minded to be accorded the treatment due to their ordinary clients. Still I had become used to him and defied prejudice. When alone in camp I could at least tell him of my point of view and he never seemed to disagree which was more flattering than most of the people I met.

On one of those trips I had been in Arizona and returned to the Cananea by train. As Ben and I made our way to the hotel I saw in the sky the promise of one of those torrential rains which are so common in Northern Sonora. If I had been ordinarily alert I would have hurried to the livery stable and left at once for Bicoachi. I was tired and perhaps dumb from over-indulgence in Arizona hospitality which is demonstrated by liquors strong and potent and in such mind felt little desire for a thorough drenching. When the rain ceased (which it did as quickly as it began) I got my horse and started homeward, as I had anticipated the first ford was a flood and there were yet some fifteen more to negotiate before making Bicoachi. At the ford there were several mounted Mexicans evidently debating whether to make the passage. If an American wanted prestige he could show no weakness so I passed through their group with a greeting and plunged in. The waiting Mexicans followed me across, and at each succeeding ford we picked up two to five hesitating Mexicans until at noon I found myself the leader of a cavalcade of about 40 of my neighbors. About 3:00 in the afternoon we had made another crossing by swimming and when safely across I heard yaps of distress and looking back I saw the current had landed Ben in the roots of a tree and was holding him there powerless. The tree was midstream with the butt toward the flood, the roots being stretched out like the tentacles of an octopus, and it was into the maws of this inanimate beast that Ben had to get caught. I hesitated awhile but his distress decided me, and going up the bank on my side I pushed off into the river again and allowed myself to drift down against the tree roots and join Ben. After extracting him and making safety on the bank I suddenly realized by the demeanor of my escort that I had done myself more service than I had imagined. They were positively reverent in their comment on my rescue and although they questioned my good sense in considering a dog worth risking anything for, I quickly saw that the idea of coveting my saddle or gun at the expense of a blowing with the owner had left their minds forever.

Alan, Bicoachi, Mexico 1902
ARH archives, editor

8

Dog-Gone Memories

The Home Lot

When an old man who has been much bitten by Wanderlust summarizes his experiences, he is much surprised at the influence that chance dogs have exercised in the none too placid transit of his life's span. Personally I now realize I owe dogs a considerable debt of gratitude for the understanding and sympathy they have extended to me when often the same qualities were denied me by my fellow mortals. I therefore desire to record some of these memories and the circumstances surrounding our relationship.

I belong to a dog family. There were packs of dogs; my Mother had her dog; my brothers had their dogs; I had my dog; and when a guest arrived he generally added one or more.

At the age of eight to discuss mange or distemper was nearer our hearts than verbs or nouns. I don't think we were very gentle kids; indeed, I think it is possible we were a little tough, but we did love dogs.

At that age, I judged a dog's worth by two characteristics: Breed, and ability to fight. Under this rating my elder brother had the pick of the bunch – Tartar by name. A cross between a bull and a fox terrier. All he knew was fight and love of the kid who would introduce him to more of his desire. With no dog fight in sight he could be persuaded to fill in his time by harrying the neighbors' cats, and if these natural desires were temporarily curtailed he was liable to get into mischief by chasing stock or worrying a stranger whom he thought was a trespasser. Could there be anything more desirable to a boy's mind? Not mine. I traded brother out of him. He cost me most of the material things I possessed, but I had what I valued more – Tartar.

In a few weeks we cemented a strong friendship; I could climb a tree which grew in our yard and enter a second story window and Tartar, even if it kept him there all night, would sit at the foot of the tree until I came to relieve him of his vigil.

When I swaggered down the village Main street there might have been dogs in sight when we hit it, but as we progressed down the line, of dogs there were not. I lived in Tartar's reflected glory.

Many and glorious expeditions Tartar and I took extending our fame through outlying and distant villages. Sauntering as Fink, "Not calculating harm but curious" to see if the natives considered they had dogs of the fighting breed. Or with no further fields to conquer we were in the woods after rabbits and squirrels; I armed with a shotgun and Tartar, my trusty aid securing the trophies.

There was a Scotch gardener employed by the family who among other things raised hothouse grapes. He and I had a difference of opinion regarding the quantity of said grapes to which each member of the family was entitled. Resenting this authority, I determined to raid the vines on my own account. Also being of that age, such an important act of piracy could only be done after dusk. Although there was nothing to keep me from going out through the front door, to be in keeping with a true burglar, I must use a rope ladder from my window. Climbing the ladder after successfully making the foray, I threw my arm over the sill, but Tartar guarding my bed must have been awakened too suddenly for with a spring he fixed his teeth in my wrist. I nearly fell to the ground with my loot, but the moment I shouted he was all penitence. I was made to feel that I had committed a breach in our comradeship and owed an apology for not taking him along. I did my best to square myself for making the expedition alone and except for an occasional look of reproach our understanding was renewed.

At the age of fifteen, I sailed to Brazil to be gone two years and we parted. Tartar now suffering from age, became morose, making no new friends. Eventually it was necessary to chain him to a kennel but his disposition went from bad to worse. Lunging at everybody and everything that came within striking distance, he was a menace and had to be killed. When I heard the news in my exile, my grief was real, and in my sorrow I vowed never again to love another.

A Nomad in Wyoming

I was to wander the next ten years through Texas and Colorado, punching, railroading and mining and my affections were given mostly to horses who have many traits in kinship with humans, and I hit Wyoming in the '90's. *(1890's)*

Here I had discovered a gold bearing ledge which I filed on as a mining claim and was working there after the manner of prospectors, which was to periodically labor on an established mine, and when a grub-stake was secured, return to one's holdings fortified with a stock of beans, coffee and powder and work feverishly until one of the essentials was exhausted, which gave one no other alternative but to hike back to the source of original supply.

On a trip to the County seat for grub and human contact, I was wandering between those social centres wherein such as I were welcomed with hospitality and warmth, when I became conscious that I had a companion. A very old hound dog was deigning to notice me without my spending money on him. As this was the first living thing in town that had thus honored me I stopped to size him up. As he stood in the snow for the inspection I had to admit to look at he was – not much dog. Besides being old, age or mange had taken all the hair from his back; he was also big, which is a terrible drain on a slim larder; but what did stick out was he was friendless, so was I. We had a bond and I encouraged him to follow me to the first saloon where I got him some sandwiches from the free lunch counter, and judging by the way he gulped these, it was his first meal for days.

My new friend was no stranger in town. I was told that his name was Reg. He had belonged to a telegraph operator who had died and none cared to give him a home on account of his age. I decided to remedy this condition. He could be no hungrier with me than he appeared to be in town, and at least we had a shelter from the snow.

Reg tagged me back to my claims. Often we bordered on hunger; at times we preferred hunger to the monotony of beans. At rare intervals we had a debauch such as a can of salmon or a pound of cheese—not that we cared particularly for salmon or cheese except that they did not taste like beans. And molasses – one lick of Reg's tongue in a spoonful of molasses and you could not persuade him that he was not in Dog Heaven.

Our best periods for food were when I hired out to labor, the boarding house taking good care of us both, but Reg showed no inclination to linger around civilization when the time came to return to our dugout – and beans. If he had been younger he might have occasionally secured a rabbit for himself but his age handicap was against him, and they only played with him. Our fresh meat was furnished by fortunate shots at antelope that would use the spring for a watering place.

A half mile below the plateau on which the claim was situated there was a running creek upon which various cow-outfits would camp a day in their passage through the territory, and on these visits Reg shamelessly worked their hospitality. Indeed, he was so frequent a visitor to one camp that he excited curiosity, and one morning, working in my tunnel I was surprised to have a stranger walk in on me. The usual 'Howdy's' were exchanged, and then he said embarrassedly, "Say, Stranger, by the way that there dog of yours eats when he comes to camp, I guess you-alls hain't got much pickings up here. What's the matter with you coming down yourself at noon?"

I laughed and accepted in the spirit that the offer was given. He had climbed that hill to find out of there was a hungry man within range of his plenty. The West was that way those days. Slabs of fried meat and prunes tasted like something we had dreamt about; and we always carried a hunk of beef home. From then on, whenever that outfit hit the camp ground the cook would shoot his rifle and helloed until I came to the rise and waved – which meant that I could come down at noon and join Reg who was already there. On leaving, neither of us felt in any immediate need of food.

The manager of the mine where I worked for my grubstakes had been showing curiosity regarding what I possessed as a claim of my own, and I persuaded him to ride over and inspect it. After a careful scrutiny of the two-hundred-foot tunnel, he asked my price. I, trying to assume a poker-face, said, "Ten thousand dollars. Taking a pick, he went back into the tunnel to collect samples of the ledge.

He returned to my camp in less than a week and offered me for the three claims four thousand dollars cash. I declined; perhaps weakly. Then he asked, "How much?"

And he had me. I dare not got back to the original ten-thousand-dollar price, because he knew too much of my circumstances, and also by being manager of the only paying mine in the neighborhood he controlled my source of revenue. Hedging, I held for five thousand dollars. After bargaining we compromised for four thousand, five hundred dollars. Holy Smoke! I didn't even want supper.

Next day Reg and I walked two miles to the road and intercepted the stage. We travelled light—my guns, a few books, some letters and the old sewing bag was all I carried. With four thousand, five hundred dollars in sight, whoever wanted them worse than I, was welcome to the torn bedding, dirty clothes, pots, tools and the food the dugout contained. Yet as I slid down the hill I sent back a friendly glance at the old camp. It was the ground on which a long battle had been fought – and won.

That night Reg and I were guests at the Railroad Hotel and on the morrow the business was transacted so easily it appeared nearer a dream than reality. Reg and I felt we were entitled to a rest.

I should have been happy – Reg was. With Reg at my feet and

nothing to do but lounge between meals in a comfortable chair on the porch, the contrast between our present and our past suggested only content – yet, the old lure of the Wanderlust was already fermenting. Horizons were so wide—Alaska, Australia called me, but a chance article concentrated the desire in another direction. It was to be Africa. But what of Reg?

Vainly I sought him a home. He was too old, too unattractive, to appeal to anybody. I thought of pensioning him but was too sophisticated to imagine this would insure him kindness or even decent treatment. Then a druggist suggested chloroform, assuring me it was a perfectly painless death; "a-going to sleep." The very thing. I was determined to act.

Buying a bottle of chloroform one morning, and armed with a sponge and cardboard funnel, I took Reg for a walk. I had decided a deserted stone quarry situated two miles west of the town was a quiet and fitting place for a ceremony of such serious import to both of us. In our old friendly relationship, we meandered over the prairie until the quarry was reached, then we sat down for a while and communed further. To postpone the ordeal was only pain; I drew the cork, saturated the sponge and called Reg. For the first time in two years he showed suspicion of me, his instinct told him I was not a friend. I called again. No response but a questioning wag; then I scolded and he cowered. I began to dislike myself. Walking toward him he cowered lower. "Fool," I said to myself. "Why did I not bring a gun? I know what they are." Still in my cosmos there is a relentless streak. I took Reg by the neck and thrust the funnel over his head. He resisted. His pal was double-crossing him. Slowly I felt his struggles subside and finally he lay still. Sick from the drug I had inhaled myself I walked a short distance and watched. I was also sick of my job. Never had I done so cowardly an act; and never had I felt so remorseful.

Drawing myself together I commenced to bury him. I am a powerful man and I piled tons of loose stones over his form. Some of the rocks must have weighed two hundred pounds and I did not stop until he had heaped above him a pile eight foot square and six feet high. That cairn of rocks must to this day be a matter of wonder to anyone who unsuspectingly stumbles on the monument. Secretly I feared he would crawl from beneath and reproach me; and as I slowly walked town-ward I glanced back frequently to see if by chance he was following.

And that--- except for those twinges of conscience I shall always have, was the end of Reg and Wyoming for me.

War in South Africa

A few years later in Africa I had a Ben to provide a home for. Ben was mostly pointer, brown and fat. Ben, derived his name from Benjamin Schults, the master of his mother. Schults had a pet female dog who was very prolific, and he also had a complex against killing dogs, so everybody who showed any signs of sentimental dog leanings had one of her numerous and ever recurring progeny wished on him. In recognition of our weakness we, in mild irony, named our obligation: Ben. Whenever I strolled abroad there were at least ten Ben's within my ken.

Very intimate friends Ben and I were not; I was enjoying a period of prolonged prosperity and the quality of our regard for each other was in no way tested. Ben's mission in life was to find a shady spot on the porch wherein to lie between meals. And if he felt like it he sometimes gave me a friendly wag as I left or returned from my work. On Sundays he might accompany me to the tennis courts and renew acquaintance with his numerous relatives. This was practically the extent of our intimacy and neither considered the other a necessity. I was not dependent on him for companionship and he did not know he was dependent on me for food.

Perhaps fortunately for myself, this world of ease suddenly ceased. The differences between the Boers and the British broke into war, and with my usual proclivity for letting sentiment outweigh reason, I joined the Boer forces. With my house closed there was no place to leave Ben so I took him with me to the front.

In tactics the Boers introduced new methods in warfare. As the few against the many, they had to adopt a defensive strategy and our days were spent in trenches, behind rocks and bushes or any other shelter that temporarily hid us from an ever-watchful enemy. This procedure was excellent and effective, but if you happened to be burdened with a dog that ever so often considered it was his duty to see how you were getting along, it was not so much so. I would be safely ensconced behind some rock when Ben would wander over the field to discover my whereabouts, sniff me out, linger a few minutes, then decide it was time to again return to camp. Needless to say, he would thus expose my hiding place to the enemy and for the rest of the day when I ventured a head over the top it was greeted with spattering bullets. From being an appendage, Ben became something more than a nuisance; he was a menace.

War brings out the best and the worst in men. The game is to shoot the other fellow and if you can't shoot him, you shoot his horse or dog. Anything goes that carries harm to the enemy. Ben was shot at enough to kill a dozen men but never hit, and he appeared not to realize he was being shot at. It became a question of whom would get it first—he or I.

In these times of trial and in spite of his dumbness, the friendship between us became closer than in the easier days, and because we were both dependent on the other's spontaneous recognition, for six weeks I endured the danger involved, although under the circumstances it should have meant little. In camp and out he was a constant burden and threat to me. Queer things humans – they will spend their best energy trying to kill each other, yet hesitate to kill a dog that is a danger to their own lives. And I carried a pistol at my waist.

Finally the enemy shot one of us and fortunately it was he. I decided to finish the campaign without adopting another pet. Protecting myself would give me ample opportunity to employ all the ingenuity of which I was possessed.

A Gringo Looks at Mexico

Three years later I was six thousand miles from Africa and a prospector de luxe. Or to be more geographically precise, on the Mexican border in Southern Arizona. Two of us as prospectors were furnished with horses to ride when we desired, a liberal expense account, and a cook and wagon so that we lost no time from the business in hand.

Gila River
ARH archive, editor

When camped on the Gila River a month after the expedition started, a stranger wandered in and showed an inclination to linger. He was a brown, curly haired spaniel who had evidently found an ample food supply in the rabbits, snakes and lizards furnished by the country, but was hungry for human company and willing to make our wagon his headquarters if it suited us. We welcomed him as a guest. As far as we knew there was not a habitation within fifty miles of us.

In a few days he selected me for his more intimate attention and accompanied me when I left camp on the daily ride or tramp in the vicinity. The outfit drifted slowly along, crossing the Mexican border and as the dog had now become another habit of mine, I named him after my last attack – Ben.

In a period of months we travelled hundreds of miles, carefully going over the geological formation of the country through which we passed. Ben, always my attendant, demanded a certain amount of care when he got in situations he could not control, but was responsive when relieved of his difficulties. One of his great trials were the dead cactus limbs. When following me he would collect the needles in the pads of his feet and then attempt to pull them out with his jaws. The consequence was disastrous, and there was for him no alternative but to sit down on his hind quarters and howl for help. I, intent on my own business was perhaps a mile away, and had probably forgotten his existence; but on hearing his appeal I'd return and relieve his feet, and he could again follow until he stepped on another bunch. In camp after supper he kept me from being better employed by asking me to pick stickers from his tongue and jaws. Yet no persuasion would induce him to voluntarily stay in camp with the cook; he wanted to be in on all that was doing.

Thirty years ago, Northern Sonora in Mexico was one of the best game countries imaginable. Brown bear, deer, wild hogs, mountain lions and herds of wolves gave Ben and I adventure aplenty; as these encounters were not deliberated but in the ordinary course of attending to our duty the interest for us both was accentuated from having been unsought. Our mining activities finally centered on working four claims which were widely separated. The extreme Southern prospect was 150 miles over the Mexican border and the Northern limit, 90 miles above the American line. Between these widely scattered prospects I was constantly on the road utilizing many forms of transportation including saddle horses, railroads and stages, and always accompanied by Ben.

To know what it meant to have a dog as a traveling companion you have to know something of the point of view regarding dogs of those with whom you came in contact. Mexicans had no comprehension of dog companionship or understanding of those who found a value in it. Hotel men considered money collected to feed a dog was a legitimate tax on the weak-minded and implied no obligation. To baggage men it was purely a source of revenue, and stage-drivers thought anyone who insisted on a dog riding instead of running in the stifling heat was entitled to pay two fares for being a sap. When you consider that to start from the Southern claim to get to the Northern, I rode sixty miles on horseback, a night in a hotel, ninety miles on trains with three transfers and two stop-overs, --- including negotiating terms with three baggage men; then another night in a hotel and next day on the stage topped with a fifteen mile ride in the saddle, you will see my traveling companion was some responsibility. Yet when I thought of the lonely Mexican trails, the payrolls I packed, the slight value Mexicans placed on a human life, particularly if it rode in a good saddle, I was grateful to have someone along who might sense when we were not alone, even if I thought we were.

Ben and I shared many adventures on lonely trails and although he was always a comfort to me, at times I was useful to him. I remember being caught in one of those semi-tropical rainstorms that suddenly put the rivers in flood, and I was following a trail that for twenty miles constantly crossed the stream bed. At the first ford I found a few Mexicans undetermined whether to tackle it or not. To an American operating in that territory it was unwise to show hesitation in a tight place. I greeted them, rode through their midst and plunged in. They followed. At each successive crossing I picked up a few more undecided natives until I had collected a formidable cavalcade. At one of the crossings a tree had been thrown down and its roots reached upstream like a spider's web. Into this trap the current hurled Ben and because of the pressure of the water he could not extricate himself. He howled his distress. There is always a price to friendship --- even a dog's friendship. Perhaps that is as well, or it would not be so valuable.

I rode two hundred yards up the stream and dropping off drifted with the current to the tree and released Ben. When we reached the bank I noticed looks of astonishment from my escort, but I did not at the time realize how important an incident had occurred in my affairs. I learnt in the next few months I had been rechristened. I was now "Dog-man" and it symbolized luck for me, because they reasoned that there was some infernal contract between my dog and I, and a man who would do for a dog what I had done, would be dangerous medicine to tackle for small change. I think this incident was a good deal responsible for me having the freedom of the territory during my stay.

As a nomadic existence our life was perfect – ever moving, abundant game, some danger, and except for our employer, no obligation; but it was not to last forever. The rosiest picture has its shadow. The Mexicans started one of their periodic rebellions. Difficulties multiplied – my men couldn't be kept working, and the mines had to close. Disliking to lose a job that so thoroughly suited me I wanted to stay and argue but

I knew it was not wise for an American to seek an argument with a Mexican revolutionist, so I took the course of reason and retired over the border to our Arizona mine. Here again we were not to linger long. The New York agent sold the mine under our feet and once more I was adrift on the world.

Knowing myself, it was certain I would skip at least a thousand miles before again locating. I arranged a home for Ben with a manager; took a strained farewell of my old friend and got on the train for California.

Making a Home in California

Rest and time helped me form an opinion -- I was an embryo rancher. With this conviction firmly fixed I bought a place in the Coast Range, one hundred miles South of San Francisco; a brush covered plateau which I figured would make ideal fruit land because it commanded a magnificent panoramic view of many square miles of valley and timbered hills. You know what I mean -- it would be pleasant to work it into as good a ranch as it was possible to make it, and it was the pleasure of doing it that I was after.

Here I found abundance of work: woodchopping was my "profession"; grubbing roots and building roads my pastime. The proceeds from the wood furnished me plenty to eat and a liberal reading account, but at times I was lonely – for a dog.

I traded at the County seat six miles to the South, and made a few acquaintances, one of which was a lady who told me she was in distress. Her dog had formed a chicken eating habit and her husband, tired of paying an extortionate charge for the victims, had told her that she had to get rid of her dog. I went over to look at it, or rather her, because it was a female. She was a black, silky coated cocker spaniel.

I said I would take her and soon cure her of her weakness for chicken. The lady threatened to take her away from me if I was cruel to her. I said she certainly would not, because I didn't intend to train dogs for someone else. Finally she was convinced that I would treat it with ordinary kindness and the exchange was made. With the dog's leash I was also offered a comb and brush. These I declined. From now on she was going to attend to her own toilet. Then, I was informed her name was Paloma. Ye gods! That was Spanish for "Dove" and although it might fit the bearer it was hardly suitable to a person with my rather rough bearing and appearance to be followed by a dove. No! I would change it to Loma, which meant mountain; this of course didn't classify the dog but it fitted the man and his home.

Three times Loma killed a chicken on me; three times she received a severe whipping, this convinced her that killing chickens was no fun anyway. For the ten succeeding years we never had anything that approached a serious disagreement. As a companion she was under all circumstances perfect. Together we slowly developed a home. We took our work seriously and play blithely. When Loma considered it was past a meal hour she would make a mild protest and start toward the cabin to shortly reappear with another appeal against overtime. Stacking the tools was the signal for wild glee, and warming the cabin and getting supper, further excitement. Our play had many angles. The surrounding county was picturesquely beautiful and we took excursions with our lunch to every knoll or hill within a radius of twenty miles of the home. We also occasionally visited in town, choosing houses to which we were both welcome. I was astonished at the reasoning with which Loma figured out a line of conduct suitable to all occasions. On the ranch, night or day she was all alertness. Nothing was allowed to move within or without the house without an alarm. Nothing approached us in the woods without warning. Yet this same dog would lay quietly in someone else's living room absolved of all responsibility; or when I smuggled her into my bedroom in a hotel she assisted the strategy with wonderful cunning. Instead of skipping along the corridors she would walk in such a way that even her claws did not make a sound on the hardwood floors. Each passed door she knew was a threat, and once the sanctuary was reached no excitement or noise in the passages made her forget the necessity of caution. And if I was theatre hungry, I could lock her in the room with any piece of my personal belongings, and I knew when I returned she would still be undiscovered.

Such was the beauty of our homesite, it attracted many people from the city, some of whom stayed to become friends. Frequently there were offers to entertain us in the city in return for our hospitality, but I patiently explained we felt nearer our own setting when at home. But there is always a weak spot in every situation and one time the picture painted for my beguilement was so alluring that I consented to make the trip. With growing apprehension, the time to start grew closer. A journey of so much moment entailed radical departures, not the least was spending the woodchopper's fortune in raiment that would furnish him with an obvious disguise in imitation of sidewalk initiates. Before we knew it, Loma was in the care of the baggage man and we were on the train bound for San Francisco. For fifty miles my well-meaning friends expatiated on all they would do to entertain me. I was to meet this and that person; hear concerts I knew I would not understand, and slowly it bore in on me that I was an emotional fool who had given away to another of his weak impulses.

While waiting at a side track, what seemed like a long time, the conductor passed through the car and someone asked him the reason of the delay. He replied, "We are waiting for the up train from San Francisco." Here, I immediately recognized was a message sent to me direct from heaven. Hastily I announced that I had forgotten an important engagement on the morrow at the ranch. In the face of surprise and incredulity I said thanks and goodbye; grabbed my bag; fled down the aisle; raced up the side of the train; salvaged Loma from the baggage man and caught the other train just as it pulled out. Without a ticket, and Loma under my arm, I, bound homeward, took refuge in the smoking car. The conductor accepted my fare and explanation, and, to her joy, allowed Loma to ride on the seat with me. With a sigh of relief, I settled down to the knowledge we were now headed in the right direction.

What were the feelings of my would-be hosts I could only surmise. Very naturally they were hurt, but from consideration of the time given me for action and the desperation of the situation I took the best way out. I knew their final conclusion could be nothing else than that it was fortunate for them the break occurred before they had sponsored me in a wider circle – perhaps the story has become an example of the care one must use in cultivating the society of roughnecks.

Capt. Alan R. Hiley with Loma
ARH archive, editor

That night after dark, Loma and I were dropped off the train two and a half miles from home. Either one of us could have found the cabin blindfolded. To make the joy of the return keener I tried to imagine something had happened to the cabin in our absence, -- nothing had. Even the air was better than any other air in the world. With a supper of canned goods and crackers, Loma and I wanted nothing but to snuggle in for the night. For us—this was the life!

And so the years passed. Loma aged, grew greyer around the muzzle, moved more sedately, groaned when she turned over. She was getting ready to quit me. Never had a dog been a more loyal companion. Masefield said somewhere of a dog:

"Damned by a dog's brute nature to be true."

When you repeat this you have said all that Loma represented to me.

Tragedy was stalking us. Loma developed stomach trouble, probably from some long-forgotten bone. Slowly she faded, suffering much and eating little. If she had been a lesser dog, I should have put her out of her misery but I could not force myself to this act of mercy. Painfully I waited in suspense until grateful to us both the end came.

Shall I ever have another pal? I don't know. I buried her at the base of a redwood tree and around her grave I planted peach seeds from which I got two trees. The fruit grown on a tree nurtured by her warm heart should be sweeter than any other variety. I know that they will be to me.

My home is so closely associated with memories of her that for ten years I have felt disinclined to allow another canine to trespass in territory so strictly hers. Every foot of road, every grubbed acre, every neighborhood trail, the porch to the shack—her enlarged portrait looking at me from the wall with pensive eyes, are all eloquent of her sway.

And yet—the desire to be loved is a universal one; and I'm too full of faults to fill a human ideal. At sixty you know your own shortcomings and have settled down to try and live amicably with them. Fellowmortals deem it necessary as an illustration of their own perspicacity to remind you constantly of your fortune in receiving their notice or consideration. I never knew a dog that regarded poor grammar or an unshaven chin as a barrier to harmony. There is some thrill when you can drop your hand on a chum's head and feel the vibrations of his responsive wag. Who knows? Perhaps someday a forlorn ki-yi of no breed, dusty, hungry and road-weary will drop off the highway seeking food and peace; and meandering up to my cabin give me that look which says, "I'm lonely; how are you?"

And I shall give back the same glance I receive and answer, "So am I. Stick around."

A Fading Hill-Billy

But this was many months ago—nevertheless I wrote as a prophet. The ki-yi is here and this is how it happened:

I had been down to the local store and Post Office *(Felton)* and was making the home hike with two dozen cans of milk, fifty cents of sugar and assorted sundries slung in a gunny sack over my shoulder. The distance is two and half miles, the load was heavy and I was anxious to gain shelter as there was a dreary drizzle slowly wetting me.

Halfway on my route home a small mongrel of the Scotch terrier type came from a yard and sniffed my heels ingratiatingly; curiosity—I thought, but a second glance suggested otherwise. He was no breed, mostly white with a few black spots, and his very closely curled coat was a pathetic mat of tangled filth proclaiming aloud his neglect. Clouts of dirty hair as big as a hand danced on his back as he trotted by my side. He was playing me as a forlorn hope.

As we passed the homes scattered along the highway I watched as he curiously intruded into each yard, quizzically giving the layout the once-over and returning to me again as his best bet. It was evident he did not belong to a local family.

A car dashed by us and he tangled in my feet avoiding it, showing he had been on the road some time and learnt protective sense from cars. The next car that past going our direction, he dashed after; his short legs fast losing distance in the race. Ah! I thought, he recognized either the car or somebody in it. Completely mistaken. After chasing it two hundred yards he stopped abruptly and trotted back to meet me. His proud air said plainly, "I made that one run. Didn't I scare it?"

When we arrived at the foot of the hill where I leave the County Road to ascend a mile to my perch on the mountain side, I eased my load from my shoulder in the shade of a cottage porch situated at the junction. The woman came out and exchanged the usual courtesies and then saw the dog. "Is that your dog?" she asked.

"No," I replied. "He's a stray."

"Well, we have too many dogs come here," she said angrily, and waving her arms threateningly, with raised voice she scolded the waif until in fear he tucked his tail and forlornly started over the road we had come, casting back regretful glances over his shoulder.

In the drizzle, dragging his feet in slow progress about one hundred yards, he found a six-inch wall to a culvert draining the road. Sheltering himself behind this in plain view of us, he laid down in the wet, and propping his head over the top of the wall he looked at me – and nothing articulate could have said any plainer, "Peter, you have denied me!"

I swung my load on my shoulder to proceed up the road; then I turned, and whistled; delightful abandon – renewed hope. Up, up we went through the wooded trail. No alluring side trips for him; closely he hugged my heels. "I don't know where you are going," he said, "But your destination is mine – lead on."

With an occasional rest we reached the cabin; I threw open the door and flopped wearily on the couch. Ki-yi followed me in, showing no curiosity of what was or was not in the house; what was there or not there he accepted. Dropping on the floor at the foot of the cot, he dropped his head on his fore paws and from one visible eye, stared at me for ten minutes without even the motion of an eyelid. To him the important question of "to be or not to be" was still unsolved.

Rested, I got up; lit the drum stove, put on the coffee and started our lunch. This consumed, the tail slowly wagged in peace by the stove. He had arrived at journey's end. Then to start the day's business, I got out the shears. Of all the vocations I had tried out in the past, sheep shearing was not included, but this dog had to be sheared. Nothing could enjoy life in this filthy condition; even one eye was matted shut. How he got in such a state was a matter of surmise. Perhaps he had annoyed some irritated person, who had thrown a pan of greasy water on him, or for protection he may have crawled under some car, or laid on a dirty floor in a garage. No matter the cause, it had to be remedied. Placing some papers on the floor by the stove, I laid him on his side and started action. I uncovered an eye nearly lost in a screen, cut loose clots of hair as large as tennis balls and threw the refuse I gathered by handfuls into the stove. For one hour he endured my clumsy efforts patiently, during which he was repeatedly rolled around to give me the greatest advantage in my endeavors. He knew, in spite of tears, punches and pulls I was doing him a service, and there was no protest by sound or action. Pounds of dirty wool went in the stove and it was not without animal life. The shearing concluded I still had to remove innumerable wood-ticks that had found refuge in the mess, immune from every effort he could make to protect himself.

When through I put him outside and he frolicked frantically. He had thought that never again would he feel the freedom he was now enjoying or have the opportunity to protect himself from the parasites he had harbored in his tangled coat. He certainly looked a different dog, although to anyone but the dog and myself the job did not entitle me to any laurels from the barber union. I didn't want any. I was better suited while he romped to take a bath and a change of clothes.

That night I made him a box bed of gunny sacks in the woodshed. When ready for sleep I introduced him to it, and he accepted it gratefully. Scarcely in bed, I heard a wild disturbance and sprang up alarmed. What was wrong? Ki-yi was madly rushing in every direction barking pugnaciously. I was puzzled; I could understand with our numerous animal life that something could disturb him, but why in so many directions at once? And then I drew on my knowledge of dogs and understood. He was telling me, "All right, Old Scout, you go to sleep. I have taken charge out here."

Next day I gave him the needed bath. He became a clean and rather good-looking dog until he rolled in the mud which to a dog's point of view is the finishing touch to a bath. Although I didn't think it improved his appearance he was so proud of being able to assist me in his toilet, that I forgave him.

For a few days he took in the dimensions of the new domain, ascertained the boundaries, and made up his mind what did and did not constitute a trespass; and as we are now co-owners nothing is now allowed to approach without he warns his partner. The rake of his stumpy tail has ascended until it is nearly vertical. A plutocrat never had more of the property sense than this new side-kick of mine. This is no more a few acres of clearing in the brush, it is a gentleman's estate – or rather, the estate of two gentlemen.

Old bones that I have wastefully thrown away are now industriously collected and cached for what lean days may await us. The third day in possession, Jerry – yes, his name is Jerry—made his first contribution to the family larder. With a good deal of strut, but not quite certain of his ground he came from the brush bearing a full-grown cottontail rabbit. I hurriedly reassured him. I'm fond of fried rabbit.

And together we go to work in the woods or the roads as the need demands; and of rights there appears no question in his mind. We are partners. His manner says, "You're over sixty, I'm one. A suitable age for such an alliance. We'll just get old together. How about it Pal?" And I answer him in dog language, "Righto! Let's go!"

And we will.

9

Prospecting Before Gasoline Came

In casting back to those days when automobiles were unknown one's mind lingers affectionately on the Prospector and his manner of life. It is a question if society did not suffer some loss when progress in changing the order of things caused him to also change his methods or seek new fields, and this old timer become a matter for history.

This intermediary between the working mine and nature was noted for rugged courage and represented some of the choicest of the American pioneers, and he is worthy of more than a passing notice from those who would record the best of the West.

In the ranges where twenty-five years ago the prospector packed his food from eighty to two hundred miles, an automobile now brings supplies and reaches within a few miles of what were the most inaccessible spots in the United States. Today they have grand pianos and phonographs where we thought ourselves lucky if we got beans.

The old timer with wages earned after the manner of those who work underground, started to the hills to seek the prospect in its virgin state, and by his labor to develop it sufficiently to convince a capitalist that he had found a value. As a class these men have suffered undeserved through lazy and indifferent persons within the ranks, and thus discrediting the main body, but the real workers have truly earned and deserve attention for their courage and fortitude. Like the cowpuncher, and possessing similar virtues and prejudices, they have now drifted before the wave of civilization.

Bret Harte won fame for himself and the miner by his stories, but he has stressed the excesses of men who were lawless more than he treated the cause of the overt acts and their relative infrequency. The impulse to riot in these prospectors was gathered during the months spent in lonely and weary labor; a life even more solitary than that of the sailor or cowboy, who at least had companions with him on ocean or range.

I can write this with understanding on the subject of the reactions of miners in the towns, because I have felt many of their hardships, and when saturated with loneliness have joined in their excesses. Under the circumstances, it appeared to be the only available outlet for an expression as remote as possible from the complaint we wished to cure.

Those who knew the genuine gold seeker saw in him the power of human faith evidenced by the most extraordinary proofs. Few men, from those who own the mining stock to many of those who actually work in mines, have any conception of the trials that the same ledge probably cost a portion of fellow mortals called, "Prospectors."

Everyone in the least familiar with mining has heard fascinating stories of phenomenally rich strikes which have brought to their discoverers a fortune so magnificent that it appeared unjust, but a type of man which should be introduced to those unacquainted with him is the prospector who expected perennially to make a strike and was as continually disappointed.

The struggle to secure the necessary material to proceed step by step; the heartfelt disappointment when the lost months proved a worthless drudgery; the interminable diet of bacon and beans, coffee and bread, might well awaken sympathy from those who calculate cost. He was invariably an impecunious fighter for something more independent than the living wage, and as continually thrown back to a necessity of merely wage-earning again. The course of procedure of prospectors varied little.

Primarily they were miners who labored periodically in the established mines, their periods of work varying. Without rigid economy their accumulated savings of a year might equal but enough to pay for a few months' food in advance. With this he prepared to cast himself adrift in the open country and test endurance and fortune. The prospector was that miner who had more ambition than his comrades, and such a one naturally reached for some method to utilize his acquired knowledge with profit to himself.

When the supplies became exhausted, these men would leave their cherished prospect, and after another period of labor in the mines long enough to earn sufficient money for their needs, they would return to their claims to again deny themselves every indulgence in food and clothing, that this mine (a creation most often of imagination) should be fed and developed by pick and powder. And even when the weight of common sense compelled them to acknowledge the futility of further labor in that location their elasticity was generally enough that when they took to the mountains for solace with the anguish of disappointment yet on them, it was only to discover another site they considered of more promise than the one abandoned.

Pathetic enough on the whole, were it not for the triumph of hope, was this occupation of prospecting. But the nightly joy of the man who saw his next day's work drawing him so many inches toward a goal – that to him was real. It was an emotion not given to the daily wage-earner.

Hardships in living were theirs and many dangers. Things that would make an ordinary individual shiver with apprehension were to them all in the day. Fuse was expensive and a few inches saved on each blast meant extra days of uninterrupted work. As the financial situation became more desperate the shorter the fuse, and a misstep or broken rung of a ladder ended many a dream. Then in some fields there was gas, and insensible partners to be rescued, often under heroic condition. Deeds denoting high ideals, but they were not only unsung, they were treated as an incident to be expected at any time, and in no way extraordinary. Rotten and extemporary heisting ropes; falling buckets and rocks; insecure timbering and joists; all of this went with the work, and many accidents occurred through these pathetic efforts to stretch the dollars beyond their limit. It was, they thought, the only way that the goal could be achieved, and therefore – fate. Another started work where the injured or killed relinquished it. The supply of hope seemed eternal.

I once discovered an old prospector in a region outside of the mineral belt in Southern Arizona, lavishing his best strength on a dyke of Gunnison granite that would have broken the heart of a stone man. I was crossing a barren strip of sixty miles on horseback and striking a small arroyo which held a promise of water for myself and horse. I left the road and was picking my way up the creek looking for something wet, when I saw fresh workings on the hillside. Discovering water in a few yards, I turned from the creek to investigate as the purchasing of mines was my particular business on this journey. On arriving with some labor at the first tunnel I was surprised at its length and the amount of work. No trace of mineral could I see in the digging except the usual iron stain with which the country is drenched. I puzzled to decide for what purpose the tunnel had been driven; an irrigation project seemed as much suggested as the seeking for ore. A search for something was certain, but what I could not determine. Other diggings soon disclosed themselves, enough in all to represent many years hard work for an experienced miner, yet nowhere could I find quartz indicative of values in the precious metals. Thoroughly mystified I sat on the edge of one of the dumps debating the question in my mind, when the squeak of a wheelbarrow struck my ear and I started toward the sound. Dragging my horse across two intervening draws, I saw the cause of all my perplexity. An aged man had just wheeled a load of dirt from a tunnel and was stopping to breathe the fresher air. He was tall and thin, dressed in the usual red undershirt and blue overalls of the miner. His straggling white hair and beard, with the pallor of his thin face formed a striking contrast to a red "sock" cap which was worn pulled down to his ears. Struggling with my reluctant horse down to the platform on which this "find" stood, we introduced ourselves. Sam Bell was about seventy-five years old, although he carried himself with the vigor of a younger man. Learning the business I was on, he was glad to trustingly display everything he had. We first inspected the work he was then engaged upon, a tunnel of about 100 feet, which showed nothing but the familiar iron stain.

I glanced several times at my guide expecting to see some sign of insanity. The old man explained that he was following the stain and believed it to be a true fissure vein which would widen into a gold bearing lead, and he was obviously disappointed that his predictions were not confirmed by my opinion, but in a few minutes he had apparently reassured himself, no doubt with comparisons disparaging to my mining knowledge.

We went to each and every piece of work he had done, over an area of several claims, through many tunnels and cross-drifts in granite. Each of these, consummated with months of labor, showed little more prospect of gold than the rock of the New York subway. Each had been the foundation of all his hopes for the working period, to be forsaken for another lure. Bell while explaining his reasons for the starting and desertion of each, would emphasize his certainty that the next few feet of the present work must break into that expected body of ore.

If you failed to shake the faith of the average prospector in his claim, even after he had been confused technically, his general reply was, "You think with theoretical learning you can see further under the ground than a man who has been at the bottom of a hole all his life, but you can't dig with books."

As an excuse for his existence he had to believe that he would strike paying rock, and also that it was just a certain number of feet deeper. If you still bore down on him with reason until the hopelessness of further work on that particular piece of ground was proven to him, he could reassure himself by telling you, "Well, if this lead I'm following should play out, the indications show that the main body of ore is thus and thus, and I shall uncover it around here yet."

Such faith redeems stupidity and much else besides, and when Bell's offer to sell the property for $60,000 was gravely refused, he equally gravely but courteously conveyed to me his impression that my firm was perhaps a small outfit, and gave me his advice of where I could make an investment within the bounds of the limited capital apparently available, though he added, I could not expect to purchase for a small sum, anything which looked so much like a mine as his property.

With an invitation to dinner, the old man as an inducement opened his lunch bucket and disclosed a sticky mess of beans in the bottom of the can under a few soggy looking biscuits. With a hand shake, I left, wishing him both joy of his lunch, and luck with his claims. I rode back to the trail whereon I knew I could make a cattle ranch within a few miles, and was hoping that the fare would prove more appetizing than that which I had refused.

That night over a cup of coffee with my host, I found probably the only living human being who took any interest in the prospects of Sam Bell, and this with the cynical toleration the cowman generally used to the miner. Bell I learned, had persistently labored in one spot for nine years. He left his treasure for some other camp only to earn a pittance for absolute necessities in food and working material.

The mutually contemptuous attitude of the two bodies of pioneers, the miners and cowmen, was remarkable because their similarity of temperament differed only in the traits each had acquired from his calling. Yet their intolerance of each other always presupposed that each class still regarded the other as next in importance to themselves, and as such, fit associates in an emergency, when all other human beings were more or less outsiders.

This particular cowman talked over Bell's trials and struggles until gradually the deep pity that a stranger would be inclined at first to feel, gave way to one of envy. "Sometime before many moons, old man Bell will be found dead in his cabin," the host remarked. "He will die as he has lived – hoping. He will fall asleep dreaming of those next few feet."

This was but one example of the intermediary between nature and the gold mine. Faith in a judgement was so firmly rooted that it would only be conquered by death. This is the virtue that made the life of the prospector endurable. It was an armor against every hardship, climatic or pecuniary, animals or hostile natives. On a frontier country, and surrounded by a perpetual history of failures, they used as boundary monuments for new claims the same stones that marked another man's disillusionment. And these new boundaries they imagined to contain buried wealth that was to place them on a pedestal of an achievement they had founded on mining lore, and built with desire. And Sam Bells were duplicated in every mineral field of the world.

Modern advancement has made many roads where before were only deer trails, but the prospector desired no such innovation to curtail his freedom for discovery. His primary investments were donkeys and pack-saddles to carry the food, bedding and camp equipment for himself and if he had one, his partner. The equipment would contain the smallest possible allowance of cooking utensils. Add to this the drilling and digging paraphernalia, provisions for from eight to fourteen weeks, and the venture, clad in new miner's boots, blue denim overalls, and a woolen shirt was ready for the trail. Thus provided, he packed his animals and started driving the donkeys before him on his pilgrimage for wealth.

This outfit, his knowledge gained by working in various mines and his unexpended monies made his whole capital. He would urge on his burrow to the first camping place full of dreams of the "maybe."

Every mining district had its own oft recounted fable of a marvelously rich mine, preferably gold, formerly discovered but abandoned from causes varying from Indians to whiskey. Thus we had our "Peglegs", the "Lost Dutchman" and "Nancy Hooks" among others. These tales were often founded on the display of a rich piece of ore by some drunken prospector, who, in a secretive manner had given an account to some friend of a man who was the friend of the man who finally repeated the garbled story. A wise person ignored these romances of mines, but passed over to the area which he considered the zone of possibility, digging here and there on likely ledges, until he satisfied himself that he had a prospect worthy of development.

Up to this time the venture had not been unagreeable in its relaxation from the semi-civilization he had left. With the camps by streams, and perhaps venison, quail, and even bear meat, life looked restful. The Prospector was elevated in the natural expansion of the surroundings. With the choice of a location affairs changed. Measuring the surface of the land desired, it was divided into claims of 1500 by 600 feet and each claim marked by monuments of rock. When the prospector had built a stone cairn and placed therein a notice claiming to be the discoverer of this lead, his further prospecting extended to a hole on the ledge not less than ten feet deep. He was now entitled by law to hold each claim so treated, until the expiration of the second fiscal year – that was supposing the month to be June, until the end of December of the year following.

Now the real grind began with a trip to the county seat where he would file his discovery notice with the recorder and expend the balance of his small hoard in further provisions, tools and powder. A permanent camp of log hut or dug-out was established at the nearest water to his contemplated work. The assessment work of ten feet would probably have shown little increased value over the rock found on the surface, and the prospector had to dig to sufficient depth to prove his confidence in the presence of mineral.

In this second outfit of supplies he had to provide bellows, anvil, also a wheelbarrow, drill tools, shovels and picks; these were primary necessities. Perhaps he might extend to a grindstone and a little lumber if his hopes were high enough. After these expenditures, the balance of dollars was invested in a bulk order of beans, bacon and coffee, with the knowledge that it was the last supply to be obtained without return to work for wages.

This rough food and the working materials were bought with comparative lavish abundance to place the day of cessation of work for lack of material at as distant a date as possible, as well as to guard against the human weakness of indulging in luxuries of food and liquor. Often the prospector "burnt his bridges" by disposing of his burros for the reason of having a small balance on hand for contingencies such illness, or assays of rock, and to be spared the constant care of herding stock within the radius of the camp.

A week or more would be spent in building a new home, digging the spring or well, and perhaps a shelter for a few scrawny chickens brought from the nearest market, probably a little journey of eighty miles or so. The camp made, the battle began. The prospector felt he was located, be it for three months or ten years, until a purchaser arrived who would see the value in the claims which he imagined them to possess, or in an extremely fortunate case, until he could open up a sufficiently rich body of ore to make the working of the property payable by its own output, for himself; or if grubstaked, for others who had become interested. Often if alone, the prospector might be able to get a brother prospector to take a half interest with him; the purchase price being the purchaser's labor.

The exploration commenced with sinking or tunneling, but his work was done with an enthusiasm impossible to obtain from a hired laborer. It would cause the prospector to work ten or twelve hours a day under trying condition; willing to use any material as a makeshift if it aided in "making feet" in the desired direction, and each day's work was closely scrutinized for increased value in the rock.

Presupposing that the prospectors were thorough miners, details were figured to the least cost, and for economy in effort the dimensions of the shaft were cut to the smallest possible working area for the larger number of linear feet. It would be tiresome to describe in detail the monotony of this life; the hopes and the failures; the fortunes touched yet lost; the labor expended and the labor wasted; the prospector forced from need to quit within a few days of a reward that others would reap; the broken-spirited, who needed time or strength to complete his task – all these were found in every locality, the setting only deviating.

The prospector's dream was that he would discover rock rich enough to make him independent of the outside capital which was regarded as the reaper of the production of his toil, courage and brains; but "money" was welcomed when indispensable, and given the "glad hand." The prospector was generally generous, energetic and ambitious, with the largeness of judgement of those unbound by circumscribed conditions.

In experience with these men, if you circulated among them, you measured the true spirit that bore them beyond the dark record of many failures to the light of the few successes. It was a field wherein the poetry of tenacious heroism is yet unfathomed; where the old struggle of man with nature, the conflict of the soul with matter was wonderfully figured, set as it was in our Western country of great desert spaces and large grandeur.

Twenty-five years ago, much of the most beautiful country in the States was solely peopled by prospectors *(ed. note: & indigenous peoples)* who were seeking rare minerals, but deeper in their natures was the unvoiced craving to be alone with the wild and ancient beauty of these great domains. Let us hope that it will never be belittled by spirits less valiant.

10

Helvetia

As "night superintendant" on the Helvetia Copper Mine, I went on at 7 p.m. and came off at 7:30 a.m. This meant I took the end of the shift that worked from 3 p.m. to 11 p.m., directing their shooting at 10:30. Then I took the entire shift from 11 p.m. to 7 a.m. and directed the work for the day shift that started at that hour. Needless to say, I had plenty to do. I would arrive at the boarding house abut 8 a.m. after my shift had eaten and gone. Then the Chinaman cook would dig me up a couple of eggs, (eggs in Arizona mining camps those days were things only to be dreamed of). Then being tired I drank much coffee. The cook had, I knew hurried his breakfast dishes so as to get a chance to sit down with me for a talk. He was a very charming old man, almost too old for the work, but full of the gentlest philosophy. Of 40 persons on the mine he was my only source of companionship. He had perfect faith that a son in San Francisco would care for him when he had lost the power to make a living. His determination to stick at the job until physically unable thus to carry his load to the end, looked very beautiful to me surrounded by rawness. I shall remember that Chinaman with gratitude to the end. I would sometimes try to tease him by suggesting his son would ditch him—it was the fashion. It fell short of its purpose.

He would with utmost faith reply calmly, "Not a Chinaman's son." Oh! The scorn suggested of the occidental.

11

Range Lore

1928

There is always a controversy of "What of the Cowboy?" and in spite of the knowledge of what the magazines say is the character of this extinct and obscure being I feel that someday the public must get saturated with imaginary and unnatural two-gun stuff, and declare for something more possible, and digestive.

Cowboys belonged with the longhorns and the longhorns belonged with the cowboys. The introduction in the Eighties (1880's) of barbed wire and graded bulls stripped him of his setting and he died a natural death.

For many years I have sojourned beyond bedsprings and kitchen sinks, and it has convinced me that, taken by and large, the chosen of the gods – judged by generosity of thought and deed, are found in the open spots. To prove this without an impossible setting is the difficulty most writers who have attempted to depict these characters for those unable to observe personally.

If it were possible to establish a reputation as a sociologist, I would make a claim that physical soundness breeds from infancy a more generous disposition. That such dispositions lured by the promise of adventure, shun the more protected methods of trade and barter, and are sustained in their choice by their inherited endurance that accepts fatigue cheerfully. By the same trait and following my argument to a conclusion: physical fitness is aiding the factory and slum in eradicating itself, because the more rugged side of existence also means the smaller wage, and consequently the inability to decently sustain its own progeny.

I would like to illustrate the cowman of the days before barbed wire with authentic anecdotes, and although they are direct, the point is needed to carry conviction, because he had to a greater degree than any other class with which I have associated, two primary virtues: a gallant, personal obligation to protect the weak and oppressed; and a disgust of gluttony, which latter manifested itself by the insult of "hawg" in comparatively mild breaches of rules which had been developed under privations. Thus, when on the rare occasions at a home ranch butter became available as a delicacy, it was an unpardonable sin to touch it while eating the meat, and to the reasonable surprise of any individual who through ignorance transgressed this law, he would be ruthlessly reproved.

In cowpunching there could be nothing less than the best physical specimens. The rigor of the life (any hours of the twenty-four were working hours – fourteen hours an easy day and then if necessary two hours night-guard, or if with a wild herd -- all night.) Yet they were happy boys and one never heard a real grouch at being abused.

How clearly stands out the picture of a bedraggled cowhand, rain pouring from his hat, saying, "What a hell of a day. Ain't it grand? There's nothing out but dawgs and hired hands."

And when on a dark, stormy night, water running down your spine and thence to the saddle and boots, you heard across the herd a dolorous voice droning,

"If I'd only listened to what Sar-o said,

I'd now be a-lying in Sar-o's bed",

you knew the singer was not drawing on a lascivious dream but painting a very correct antiphrasis to the misery he was at that moment enduring.

Ten raw bronc's broken neither to rope, bridle or saddle were an allotment to be taken with your duties, and you used these in those periods when your broken horses were resting. At this pace do you wonder a man at forty was, "Old Bill, Old Al, or Old Tom?"

In regard to shootings – such things have always occurred on a frontier, but it was a rare case when they were advertised any in advance. They were chiefly impromptu affairs in a small-town saloon, but to read the modern story you would think a year of cow life was 360 days rioting and 5 days on the range. The truth was the reverse.

We got $25.00 per month, and after we had bought the necessities in tobacco, bedding, clothes and saddle, it took us no more than five days to donate the small balance to the saloon keepers, gamblers and dance-hall proprietors. This gave us 360 days to be spent on the round-up or in the cowcamp.

I think by those familiar with the conditions I will not be thought to exaggerate when I say that forty-five years ago in the Texas Panhandle if a cowpuncher was bitten by the desire to emulate his more sheltered brother by living in a state of matrimony, his choice in that country was very nearly limited to making his selection from the members of that old, old profession.

Social conditions have changed; and in comparison to the tolerance of 1928 toward a female who indiscreetly ranges in the realm of adventure, it seems almost unbelievable that her sister in the eighties was doomed to her manner of existence more irrevocably than the matricide is doomed to the penitentiary today.

The only reprieve these women could hope for was through the portals of matrimony. If they could find a male with sufficient faith in them to buck society, they might win freedom.

In a community of six hundred miles square extending from the Indian Territory to Las Vegas, in which practically every man and woman was known to each other, there were several men who took this chance, and from, and by the basic condemnation they had overcome, they made happiness out of it.

I think few of the old timers would question that the women who tried the experiment of matrimony were treated by her former male intimates with a delicacy which rivals any chivalry of former or present times.

In the nomadic existence of the early cowman he was often sent journeys of a distance of perhaps two to four hundred miles with a string of ten or twelve horses through thinly settled country. He was compelled to make ranch houses each night where hospitality was always assured.

One of the stopping places between the Panhandle of Texas and Fort Sumner, New Mexico, was occupied by a lady of whose past there was no secret. About once a year there were many of us who used to make this shelter for a night. I imagine these visits had a uniformity which varied only in slight details.

You rode up; (strangers were always welcome in lonely places,) and hollered, "Who-e-e!"

Amy came out. You greeted, "Howdy, Amy?"

"Howdy, Al, get down and turn your horse loose."

You took your bed from the pack horse and carried it into the house. You retailed the country-side news as Amy prepared supper, and the conversation was as commonplace, if a little more animated, as any overheard on a streetcar. It may have been that Amy and you had in the past been exceptional friends. You may have been comparative strangers. In the first event, it was not allowed to color the conversation. That past was dead. Amy's husband, Bill, was a man, holding up his end among men; you respected the present state of affairs as you knew Bill would have respected them if the positions had been reversed, for Bill's sake, for Amy's sake and probably for your own soul's sake.

Amy was dominated by loyalty to the man who had given her the opportunity to break away from the past, and her respect was translated into achievement.

Supposing someone had transgressed the community law, broken the code that governed the then inhabitants of that country? Well, after all we were fairly close to the raw, and I am positive that a breach of faith would have eventually cost the reckless one his life, through the husband, through a friend of the husband or through a friend of Amy's.

This house was a two-room adobe with no door between. In the primitive state of the country there were no conveniences and there were no compulsory obligations in the essential parts of life, unless you had the sense of decency to furnish them yourself, and I am satisfied that all these travelers found this sense in themselves without the opportunities of a higher education. He dug in his own morals and furnished himself with a conduct, which now-a-days would shine as an arc light. The guest made his bed on the kitchen floor and in the morning if he were not up, Amy stepped over the bed and started breakfast.

He rode on his journey after a real handshake. Both had a difficult life ahead; both wished deeply that the other would make the grade.

Abe Owens, an old-time trail boss, who had spent years driving cattle from Texas to Montana, was quizzed by a Philadelphia lady, who was his employer and the owner of vast herds. Abe was a "case" and she was gathering local color. She was well satisfied until the question, which ended Abe's social elevation and quenched her desire for further information was asked.

She had heard that there were families close to her holdings and asked Abe, "Do you know Mrs. Wright?"

Abe promptly replied, "Yes Ma'am. Knowed her for years, but not that way Ma'am."

How very shocking to a Puritanical mind—rude, boorish, coarse; it was really nothing of the kind; no class on earth ever gave more tenderness to the reputation or feelings of a woman. The trouble was Abe knew few women, but he was honestly trying to anticipate what he thought would be the Philadelphia lady's next question. There was no disrespect intended; there was to Abe no reason for secrecy in a matter of common information. Abe was telling it straight, which to his view would strike any hearer as extraordinary because he was probably one of the few. His surprise was at the coincidence that the lady from Philadelphia should have selected him of all the others to get information from. She had sounded and struck the sincerity of the West and it startled her.

An old-timer, Nat West (bless his memory) addressed everything inanimate or animate, except humans, as "You son of a B----." Some facetious younger man said one day, "Say, Nat, what is this 'Son of a B-----' you talk so much about?"

Nat pondered gravely for a few moments and replied, "I don't know, unless it's a man who steals 'love' and tells."

What buried page of his life was this philosophy dug from?

Or take the spirit that only took cash, even if somewhat hardily earned. A man named Jim was unfortunate enough to contract a then incurable disease. Medicine has made advances since those days, but then the relief was treatment at the Hot Springs, Arkansas. A yearly visit taken each winter, cost in the neighborhood of $500.00, which allowed a margin for an occasional stack of chips in a poker game—as necessary to an idle puncher as food.

Did Jim earn this money at $25.00 per month? Figure for yourself. I know for years he never missed a trip and the community on which he drew was small and not very prosperous. What one had, one gave; probably from $10.00 to $40.00; and the return? – Jim back on the Round-up each Spring feeling fine, and telling tales of the dudes he had met from the East.

Then a more personal anecdote, which aids my argument. When I went on the Plains as a youth, I did not immediately qualify as a top-man. Often I was given the duty of horse-rustler for the men. One day hearing two men arguing on the brand of a horse in my care and feeling qualified to pass an opinion on the subject, I did so.

One of the men, without moving from his sitting position, looked me directly in the eye—very directly – and drawled, "Lookee here, young fellow, when we need advice in this country we hire a lawyer. See?"

I saw! Blushing scarlet with mortification I wisely refrained from answering. The rebuke was justified.

Some years later I became warm friends with this man and found him sterling. We were in a cowcamp together on the Pecos River at a time when feeling was keen on an existing stock war. A hired gunman from Texas, named Ben, had joined the camp; and with an idea of establishing a local reputation, had looked for an easy subject and selected me. His intentions were apparent to everybody, including myself. Fearing my courage would wilt if kept too long under suspense I met, considerably to his surprise, his first offensive with the unforgivable term of the cow country – "You're a lying son of a B----."

The effect startling to all, resulted in a temporary victory to myself. This man left the insult un-resented. During the night he evidently reasoned that not only his immediate bread and butter depended on his ability to inspire fear, but also his being able to stay in the country and live. The cook woke me the next morning to tell me that Ben, (who was then with the herd) wished me to know he intended killing me when he came into camp if I did not crawfish.

Cold food on an empty stomach – particularly to one with an inherited reverence of law, and a distaste to either being killed or taking the life of another. There appeared to be three courses possible: I could kill him and move a few hundred miles but I had a strong family instinct and did not wish the stigma of an outlaw; I could weaken and apologize but I was Scotch with an intense pride; and so I decided to take the third course, which with a gunman was the equivalent to committing suicide—let Ben shoot first and then after the overt act, attempt to shoot him.

I slipped on my boots, strapped on a gun I never had made a habit of wearing, and went to the campfire—looking I imagine, not as a wedding guest should. The boys were buzzing with the news, and my friend, Joe, drew me aside, and in an even voice said, "Never mind, Al, if the Son of a B---- gets you, I'll get him."

Here was a redeeming act too fine for my power of description and done without the bat of an eyelash. In fifteen words Joe resounded the note which binds men in brotherhood. This offer was not made in heat of blood, nor made by a man half full of hootch, but came at five a.m. on a chilly morning on the New Mexico flats when courage should be at an ebb.

A fighter himself, he would not take the fight off my hands as that would reflect on my courage, but what he could do was see that none benefitted by my discomfiture. This offer also meant something in economic considerations; Joe had laboriously collected six hundred head of cattle in the past few years, which he would have to abandon, change his name and travel to another country. Yet this roughneck was willing to lay on the altar of friendship whatever he considered friendship demanded – be it his life or his property; and you could safely stake your soul he would have paid the price.

Well, there was no tragedy; Ben was yellower than then permitted to run in those parts and he left without killing anybody; but does not the story of Joe's offer sound like a standard worth preserving?

I am not trying to pick a quarrel with the readers of the modern conception of a cowboy. Circumstances control me sometimes better than others, yet everybody is entitled to a few bugs and the real cowboy is one of mine. We are all proselytes, but it would be a desperate crusade to change the cow story, as the two-gun man is not a creation to pander entirely to the tastes of the anaemic store clerks, who take their reading in stolen moments. The "Action Fans" cover all walks of life and are not only in the mills, factories and offices, but range over the mines, ranches and farms, and as long as our existence curbs in the human breast a known desire for adventure beyond the visible horizon, so long will the cowboy and miner be a medium to hang the fabric of false romance upon.

Under the circumstances and in view of these suppressed emotions, I do not even claim that all is not for the best, but my objection (and my innermost feelings are deeply involved) is that this fictitious character has been standardized, and we are going to lose the original due to the death by age of the few remaining persons who are yet familiar with him, if even any of these are capable of reproducing their knowledge in a manner convincing enough to be accepted as a portrait. I know with many of us it is difficult to control a desire to heroize the subject, but a consciousness of the present human complexes almost insists that, provided the truth were adhered to, there is a moral issue in doing so. What one should see is a more truthful account of what was a cowman's daily and often incredible endurance; an intimate record of his character and constant combat with elements and animals, and those very rare occasions when he took the law in his own hands, or was present when this was done to others. The percentage of "ornery" men in that country was a very, very small one, and such dispositions led to an abrupt finish when arrayed against numbers of a higher standard. A killing reputation was its own doom. As a snowball rolling down hill, the hostilities increased with each death. Each man killed left an increased number of friends who expected an accounting from the killer.

John G. Neihardt has pictured these details in his "Songs of the West", and 45 years ago an ex-cowpuncher, then a saloon keeper, named Charles Sirengo, did the same crudely but with truth, in his book, "Fifteen Years on the Hurricane Deck of a Spanish Bronco."

When this is said, where do we look? Has the truth been drowned in the deluge? Where is the Joseph Conrad for the range? The cow story which is history looks much as a needle in a haystack. It may exist but we scratch a lot of straw in vain. What oceans of prose are written at the subject which gives no conviction of the possible or probable. A few who have knowledge have written faithfully but meagerly, of whom Andy Adams, the old trail boss, is of the known, but unfortunately, to him, swimming a torrent with a herd, three days soaking, on a broken-legged horse miles from nowhere are commonplace, unworthy of comment. Searching for the picture, you wade through seas of schoolmarms supposed to be teaching you don't know what, dashing through the country as an example to the women who had previously filled the local field; or fair eastern heiresses who after a world search, were destined to discover their ideal at a roundup. The man on the big ranges of the early Eighties knew no schoolmarms and no schools, unless he went back to the settlements; I know I saw none, and if any heiress abducted one of the crowd it was done so subtly it was not recorded.

There is another fact beyond contradiction, that, be it for good or evil, the conception of mental cleanliness was then different to those now accepted. In these days you hear told without protest, in cars, offices and private houses, tales which in the most casual way malign the integrity of the teller himself and those related to the story, and told in a manner which gives the conviction that he himself does not think he is transgressing what a cowboy would have considered a law of decency. One time in their circle, such a breach was dangerous. Nothing is more indicative of a class than what they consider glorifying or humiliating to themselves.

I can close my eyes and imagine that someone through ignorance or daring had attempted such a cowardly slander on any woman in a cowcamp, and I see some loose-jointed roughneck slowly rising from his squatting position, and accepting what he considered was his responsibility to defend those unrepresented, he would glare into the eye of the newly discovered human, and drawl, "You sound to me like a yeller dawg."

WANTED: A historian to record the amiabilities and weaknesses, the stress and reactions of the forgotten cowboy of the Eighties (1880's). It should be a matter of pride to America. A true picture would show much to love and little to deplore.

oOo

impressions from ledger:

- Cowpunchers' distaste for cornmeal—raised on it. Each birthday had often only meant the allotment of so much "more corn to tend" (hoe).
- Learning the lost art of knowing horses' feet well enough to follow their track for hours.
- Cow puncher really a term of contempt, meant "cow prodder" or one that punched cows (or beef cattle) with a stick—and is derived from the days that cattle got so trail weary they would baulk in their tracks and refuse to move when a sharp stick was carried (or bull whip) to urge them to further effort. This was not known on the real range but in the settlements.

~ Contrast peevishness, irritability with modern conveniences and those days of tenderly nursing a smolder for hours in the hope of a warm cup of coffee—Breaking often wet cow chips hoping for a dry center or heart—nursing a few dry twigs—limited matches—using your hat or slicker as shelter—getting wet.

~ Coming home after delivering beef herd to R.R. Seeing mustang frozen in lake on plains.

~ When I got to the plains:

Independence – The post I had left I had abandoned – on my voyage seeking self-respect. I had got to this island—the sea ahead was uncharted. A little afraid - I was inclined to linger. I had for the first time on my own efforts arrived at a personal independence with surroundings compatible to my self-respect and tastes.

~ Cow chips:

Oh the fragrance.

My girl confesses a revulsion when she first saw me pick up deer dung and crumble it to ascertain the time of the deer's passing. To an ex-cowman there is positively no repugnance to cow dung—or the handling of it. He has collected it on his shirt too often to dislike its scent or touch. Further he has been benefited by its use and has an affection for it thro' association. It is the plainsman's incense. His face was tanned and his nostrils stung by its smoke and in the crowded and busy branding corral he was choked on the dust and stumbled over its material form until it becomes part of the game.

12

Sholem

First view, Glengarry Rd.
ARH archive, editor

KEEP OUT – PRIVATE ROAD – NO TRESPASS. Jim Kelly stood staring at the signs in front of him. He was winded with the half mile climb up the hill and sat down to rest. There was no mistaking the meaning of those signs – strangers weren't being welcomed with open arms. Kelly wondered why; also he wondered just what was at the end of the steep road ahead of him.

He'd find out. The owner could do no more than throw him off. His curiosity increased his speed. There was another sign – KEEP OUT. Kelly didn't ponder that one; what he craved was one look at the man who lived up a road as steep as this one and on top of it wanted no visitors.

Suddenly the climbing stopped and the road started over a plateau. Kelly was beginning to catch glimpses of the canyons below him. There it was – the cabin and smoke coming from the chimney. Kelly took a deep breath; no use quitting now. He raised his voice and called and then waited for consequences; he did not have to wait long. Out of the door of the cabin stepped a large, well-built man dressed in khaki clothes; he was gray haired with the handsomest face Kelly had seen in many a day. The owner spoke, "Howdo, Stranger, are you lost?"

Kelly started to answer, "Yes," but there was something in that face, something in the voice which said, "The truth, young fellow, is what I want and expect to get." So Kelly explained, "I'm camped at the Big Trees auto camp. I saw your signs but my curiosity got the best of me. I'm sorry."

The stern, proud face looked at Kelly intently and softened and with it the voice, "My name's McDonnell. Come on out to the Point and take a look from one of God's footstools. Wait, just a moment and I'll get the glasses."

McDonnell disappeared into the cabin and returned with a pair of white ivory opera glasses in his hand. They followed a path a few hundred feet which led past the cabin to a grove of redwood trees on the edge of the plateau.

Sholem, Glengarry Rd, 1906
ARH archive, editor

"Have a seat, young fellow," offered McDonnell as he seated himself on a trunk of a large redwood conveniently dropped just where the land began to slope off toward the deep canyon in front of them.

Then Kelly looked, and stretched out before them was a magnificent panoramic view—miles on miles of hills covered with trees and brush—here and there a green valley nestled at the foot of a hill. It was a clear spring day and Kelly had a feeling that if he had just climbed a little faster he would have caught the creator finishing up his handiwork—the artist just completing the picture with the paint still wet. Kelly sat there speechless with the beauty before him.

McDonnell broke the silence, "Will that feed your soul, son?" Jim Kelly nodded and looked at that fine face with the kindly gray eyes and started to say something. He found his throat tense so instead he looked up at the far blue hills. The old man understood.

Finally Jim could stand it no longer, "How did you find this place?"

"Well, about seventy-five, or maybe it's a hundred years ago," remarked McDonnell with a smile, "I was prospecting for gold in the Arizona desert with a partner. We had sunk a hole about a hundred feet down. We would work for about fifteen minutes then climb up for fresh air and lay panting on the edge of the hole. The heat was intense; your hands burnt when you picked up your tools. My partner entertained me by telling luring tales of cool redwoods on the banks of a river in Eureka, California, a river filled with trout. I listened day in and day out and secretly vowed that someday I would seek that country. I'd find those trees that could live for three thousand years—mind you, they were at least a thousand years old when Christ was born.

"I went up to San Francisco just after the big earthquake in 1906. San Francisco was terrible; it made one's heart sick. I decided to return to Los Angeles, but after leaving San Francisco I remembered a friend who had recently moved to Santa Cruz from Los Angeles. I changed trains to Santa Cruz. I found my friend and he was delighted to see me. He hitched up the old horse and buggy and took me up to his mountain home at the Big Trees—his place is just over that first hill we see ahead of us--- As we followed the dirt road deeper and deeper into the wooded country, I knew fate was weaving an irresistible chain. We spent a day and a night at this friend's cabin by the side of the road. It was not Eureka, but it would be my Eureka.

I returned to Los Angeles, settled up my business there and returned to Santa Cruz. I spent weeks looking for my new home. I studied maps and interviewed lots of people and finally located what was known as the "DeWald Place." This is it. It extended from the foot of the hill to the top; it was covered with brush but I guessed there would be a view from the top. Well, it took me three years to clear it and when I finished," he waved his arm at the scene before them, "I had this. It was cheap at any price."

Each sat consumed with his own thoughts for a while, when

McDonnell went on, "I had two men working for me cutting wood when I first started. One of them turned up for the first time since those days, just a few weeks ago. He is a gentle Emersonian philosopher, his partner was an Irishman named Archie. Brewer, the fellow who called on me, told me one that pleased me. Archie said to him one day, "You know Cap gets out on that Point and sits and sits for an hour at a time, just lookin' and lookin' and damned if I can see anything but a lot of hills all covered with trees."

Brewer knew what it is that holds a man to these hills. It isn't the hills and it isn't the trees. It's the peace they give you. "A Peace that passeth all understanding."

Kelly watched McDonnell's face; yes—that peace was in his soul, but below the peace were deep lines of joy and sorrow, of labor and command. And that voice – gentle, well-modulated, and yet instinctively Kelly felt its strength. What a character—a man among men, one who obviously had not started in a cabin on a hilltop and yet he loved his hilltop with a passion that held one in awe.

"Take a look at those hills with these," suggested McDonnell and passed Kelly the opera glasses. They were exceptionally powerful glasses and Kelly remarked about them.

"Yes, they're good glasses. I got them in Johannesburg thirty years ago. The Boer War was on and a friend of mine and I went to Johannesburg to equip our corps, it was the American Scouting Corp; we got everything but finally decided what we needed to round out our equipment were some field glasses. We entered a jewelry store and my pal asked to see their stock of glasses. The clerk was very accommodating and displayed all he had. We picked out two of the best pair in the bunch, one encased in black leather and this pair. My pal then called for writing paper and pen and ink. The clerk was eager to make the sale and please his customers. He brought the material—then my pal proceeded to write an order on the Boer Government in payment of the glasses. All this was done with such gusto the astonished clerk could find no words with which to protest."

McDonnell chuckled to himself, "I shouldn't be a bit surprised if that clerk was still holding the order on the Boer Government in payment of the glasses."

"My pal took the black ones," McDonnell went on, "and I these. Time and again they saved our lives. The only uncomfortable thing about these was that the sun had a way of reflecting on the gold rims and flashing a signal to the British, which until I learned what drew the sudden fire from the enemy, made things a little warm for those of us ensconced behind a rock or trench. After that I was always careful to cover the glasses with my hands before putting them over the edge to look. They originally came in a purple velvet lined case but the first rain settled that part of them. After the case went, I rolled them up in a handkerchief or a sock and kept them in my pocket."

Kelly smiled when he examined the glasses. White, ivory opera glasses trimmed with gold, pressed into service on the battlefield on the South Africa veldt. So there were fighting days in South Africa in this peaceful face? Jim Kelly looked again, "Yes, by every sign there was—an adventure!" thought Kelly to himself and that thing of Kipling's came to his mind, "Onct I was devil of a man and begad, I tuk a woman's eye." And so had this one in his day.

"Yes, boy," went on McDonnell, "I always found the chosen of the gods, by that I mean those biggest in thought and deed, in the open spaces—beyond bedsprings and kitchen sinks. I recall one fellow named Joe Splits. He was a cowpuncher on the Texas Panhandle when I went there in my youth. I did not at first qualify as a top-man and I was often given the duty of horse-rustler for the men, that is looking after the horses. One day I heard two men arguing about the brand of a horse in my care. I felt qualified to pass an opinion on the subject and did so.

One of the men, Joe Splits, looked me directly in the eye and without moving from his sitting position, he drawled, "Lookee here, young feller, when we need advice in this country we hire a lawyer. See?"

"I saw! That was the first lesson I learnt on the Panhandle---'mind your own business.'

"Some years later Joe Splits and I became warm friends. We were in a cowcamp together on the Pecos River, New Mexico. The feeling was running strong on an existing stock war. A hired gunman from Texas, named Ben, joined our camp. He looked around for an easy subject and picked on me. His intentions were apparent to everybody, including myself. I was afraid my courage would wilt if kept too long under suspense so I met his first offensive with the unforgiveable term of the cow country, "You're a lying son of a bitch."

"The effect startled everybody. Ben Kilgore left the insult pass unchallenged.

"The cook woke me the next morning to tell me that Ben, who was then with the herd, wished me to know he intended killing me when he came into camp if I did not crawfish.

"This was cold food on an empty stomach, particular to one with an inherited reverence of law and a distaste to either being killed or killing someone else. I could do one of three things: I could kill him and move a few hundred miles but I had a strong family instinct and did not want the brand of an outlaw; I could weaken and apologize but I was Scotch with an intense pride; so I decided on the third curse, which with a gunman I knew was equivalent to committing suicide: I would let Ben shoot first and then after the overt act I'd attempt to shoot him.

"I slipped on my boots, strapped on my gun—I never had made a habit of carrying one—and went to the campfire, looking I imagine not as a wedding guest should.

"The boys were buzzing with the news. My friend, Joe Splits, drew me aside and in an even voice whispered, "Never mind, Al, if the son of a bitch gets you, I'll get him."

"This offer was not made in heat of blood, not made by a man half full of hootch, but made on the New Mexico Flats at five a.m. on a chilly morning, when courage should be at an ebb.

"I've forgotten who wrote it, but 'Greater love knoweth no man than to lay down his life for his friend.' "

"A fighter himself, Joe would not take the fight off my hands as that would reflect on my courage, but what he would do was see that no one benefitted at my expense. Joe's offer meant something in cash to Joe besides taking a chance with his life. He had laboriously collected six hundred head of cattle in the past few years which he would have to abandon, change his name and move to another territory. Yet this roughneck was willing to lay on the altar of friendship whatever he considered friendship demanded—be it his life or his property and you could safely stake your soul he would have paid the price."

Kelly sat and listened enthralled and longed to have lived when days were bigger—the days when adventure and living went hand in hand. McDonnell sat and looked at the far horizon and Kelly knew well that the real McDonnell was back on the New Mexico Flats and yet through it all his spirit was serene. He had played the game of life and played it well. Kelly wondered what magic it was which gave a man of fifty that look; could one attain it or were those sort of people marked from their birth? Here was McDonnell who owned little of this world's goods and yet he lived like a king. Kelly gave up the puzzle and instead decided to find out what happened to Ben, "And what of Ben?"

McDonnell gave an indulgent grin and went on, "I met Ben out at the herd. I went up to him, looked him squarely in the eyes and repeated what I had called him the night before.

"He gulped but made no gun play. He looked at me intently for a second and walked away. It took me years to figure out why Ben acted as he did. After I had faced death many times I learnt the secret. When Ben threatened me I made up my mind to die. When he looked at me he knew I cared less for life than he did. It's a psychic thing; one you can't put your finger on, but the man who considers himself dead hold all the cards.

"Strange thing about my friend, Joe Splits—years later, I had gone to South Africa and back and was prospecting in Mexico for Cook, the mining man, I heard of a bronco rider called Joe. He rode for prizes in the fiestas and the description fitted Joe. I started to trace him. Every town I came to he had just left. This puzzled me but finally I doped it out. Joe knew me as "Texas Al" and he was being told that an American Captain was looking for him. The fact that Joe was in Mexico suggested that something might have happened over the border which made it necessary for him to spend his time in Mexico. Anyway, he did not want to meet an America Captain. I never caught up with him. I've always regretted it. I needed Joe. At that time Mexico was a pretty warm place for a gringo and I carried heavy payrolls back and forth to the mines and would have enjoyed Joe's company immensely—and it would have meant something to have touched the hand of a friend."

The sun had set. Kelly knew he had long overstayed the limit. He got up to go; took one last look at the beauty before him and held out his hand to his host, "Goodbye. This has been a privilege," and his voice went hoarse.

"Goodbye, young fellow, glad you came up. I've forgotten to ask your name but it doesn't matter. Do you see that sign on the cabin?"

Kelly read the word SHOLEM crudely printed on a board. That means PEACE, son. Goodbye and come up again.

View from the point, Glengarry Rd.
ARH archive, editor

-oOo-

One day—not long after Kelly so unceremoniously broke into Sholem another one walked up the road and came to the signs but she spent less time worrying about the signs. She was a young girl of perhaps nineteen or twenty. She also had the privilege of sitting on the Point and listening to tales of adventure until the sunset turned the far blue hills to pink and rose colors. And did she leave McDonnell the peace she found him with? Oh no! She married him.

Capt. Alan, Alan Jr, Alma Hiley July 1925
ARH archive, editor

13

Going Home

There stood that Boy again in front of the County Jail. He could not be more than nine. His young face was sullen and resentful. I smiled and said, "Good morning," but I was ignored.

Next morning I spoke again. He looked at me suspiciously but still refused to speak.

My curiosity aroused, I quizzed around and learnt that the Boy's mother was in Jail on a charge of murdering her drunken husband, whom she had killed when she found him beating her son's unconscious body. The child had been placed in the Detention Home pending the mother's trial but had escaped and made his way to the County Jail. He pleaded so pitifully to be with his mother that the very human sheriff and kindly matron agreed to keep the Boy. They allowed him to come and go as he pleased. At night he was locked up with his mother.

A week passed. I could get no response from the Boy, so I stopped one morning and told him I had some samples of drawing crayons and watercolors in my office which he was welcome to if he could use them. Again, that suspicious look, but he said, "Yes," and followed me to my office adjoining the Jail. When I got the playthings together, he grabbed them, calling a "Thank you," as he went. He had no time for formality; he was hurrying to show his mother.

We became friends after this incident and he would walk from the Jail to my office occasionally, just to pass the time of day.

One afternoon there was a commotion in the hall of the Court House – Court had just been dismissed. I suddenly remembered that this was the day the Boy's mother was on trial for her life. In the midst of all the noise—face flushed – eyes dancing – all restraint thrown to the winds, the Boy burst into my office and cried, "WE'RE FREE! WE'RE GOING HOME."

14

A Faith

1927

At the age of eighty-six years, if you have lived a comparatively blameless life, no matter from what faith you have drawn comfort, you should be entitled to preserve your peace of mind to the end. Yet a friend in this position as she nears ninety, by an accidental discovery of some Buddhist literature has for the first time in her life been thrown on the shoals of doubt, and is tormenting her short bodily tenancy with prayer to guide her feet to the right road. Here is a dilemma. It becomes a duty to remove her terror of the future so that she can have her peace of mind restored to her. So we argue thusly:

Your Oriental pamphlet received, and read with interest. There is nothing in it I would quarrel with. It is just a restatement of some old truths. The editor errs as most Occidentals when they find Oriental philosophy. Overcome by its promise they fail to consider the temperamental difference in the two people. We are not a passive people and cannot assimilate an Oriental faith in its whole. It is a process which would take generations, but there is hope that we can absorb much that will aid toward light.

To balance the spiritual values of each other, the East needs the West – the West needs the East. We can use much in Oriental philosophy.

They refuse to be disturbed with things that are to us tragedies. They know that "millions of bubbles like ourselves have already been poured and millions more will be poured in the course of time." From us they need some (and only some) of our materialistic values. Neihardt in his "Poetic Values" outlined this (in prose) better than anyone I know. He seeks a way to unite a spiritual vision with the necessary materialistic wisdom to survive in a world of struggle.

Sir Richard Burton's "Kasidah" is a splendid antidote to Occidental egoism that makes us think we are, as individuals, something of considerable importance to the scheme of things. They (the Oriental) should have part of our combativeness to overcome physical handicaps in the struggle for existence. They need something that will also inspire them into trying to leave the world better for their passage. They dream and die of inertia and starvation. We crucify our dreamers and commit spiritual suicide by a debauch of the carnal senses.

Oriental philosophy is the beginning of truth, but their passivity is abominable. Life does not imply the acceptance of existing conditions. If it is not progressive, it is nothing:

"Each hard-earned freedom withers to a bond.
Freedom is ever beyond – beyond."
                                        --Edwin Markham

The Oriental and the Occidental are totally different personalities—someday they will mingle and the best of both survive. Any why should we not recognize now as later that there are but two solutions to this rivalry of creeds and races, and these are either a benevolent assimilation or by extermination. They have mixed successfully in the past and they will, in the future do it again in spite of our present prejudices, and the sooner we get used to contemplating the idea the better for all concerned with the issue. The alternative of killing off half the population of the earth is not so pleasing and then again, which half is going to do the killing? If there is a preference I regard them as our superiors, because I judge a person or race by their measure of self-discipline:

"Take temperance to thy breast
While yet is the hour choosing,
An arbitress exquisite
Of all that shall thee betide.
For better than fortune's best
Is mastery in the using.
And sweeter than anything sweet,
The art to lay it aside."
--Louise I. Guiney

Spinoza covers everything I want for a creed in life. The divine force is in everything living – from the lowliest weed to the most enlightened human. It is the desire to live and grow – nothing more. To pass the message –to be a part of a whole – and use our opportunity to raise the level of spirituality until we become divine – divine on earth. There never was a greater dream and no man-made creed of a heaven or hell can mar its beauty.

The biblical conception of a heaven is obviously drawn to appeal to the imagination of a slave race. It did. It does. Gold and pearls. The greedy who consider themselves cheated will crave what they have not. It is easy to persuade the disinherited that gold spells happiness. Is it not sinister that gold was chosen as the symbol for deifying the home of our God? The avaricious can always be bribed, and gold to the ignorant is the source of all Joy! To them the prayer of the free soul who unexpectedly found itself in heaven is not understandable:

"God whom our father wrought
Out of their travailing thought,
Deal with us generously;
Give us our sea." -- Anne Atwood Dodge

If I thought my fate would bring me to such a comfortless place I should attempt to smuggle in a pine seedling and a sack of real dirt. I can imagine no bliss without the senses being used in its enjoyment, and a heaven without mountains and trees looks unimaginable. If I arrive conscious in any future heaven, I shall look around for some of the blest spirits I have known in this life who had never bowed to the Christian God. There was a Chinese cook in Arizona, who to me was the most beautiful spirit in the territory. There was a negress in Brazil who forty years ago nursed me when I was friendless, through a dangerous illness with a personal sacrifice that was nothing but Christ-like, and there was a Swazi native, in Africa, who when I was wounded in war, at great risk to himself, hid me, fed me and lied for me while I was sought by a power that on my capture would have stood me as a traitor against a wall. If I did not find such souls as these among the blest, I'm sure I would retrace my steps in an endeavor to discover the place for which I was better fitted.

The Oriental had the forethought to recognize that in the conception of a future existence it was impossible to ignore the senses. The senses are our present life, and cannot be wiped out as non-existent. What can be done with them and should be done with them while we are here is through purification and an intelligent guidance. Let the future of the human species be our goal. This is real. Any other faith is speculative, and a subterfuge for the true purpose of man's intelligence. The most striking contrast between the followers of Buddhism and Christianity is that while the Christian is largely concerned with a desire to force everyone to conform to their interpretation of the salvation of man, the Buddhist is indifferent to the personal conduct of anyone but himself. In the Christian's attempt at compulsory regulation there is a suggested bigotry which is offensive to those of a different faith, particularly when the personal lives and conduct of these reformers is open to question. They justly say that a prophet should be a mirror of his creed; and judged by this standard the professors of Christianity have not learnt the lesson they would preach to others. They are either ignorant of, or would purposely qualify the message that Christ by his life and teaching gave to the world.

I know that we are spiritually half formed, and that there are heights to our development yet unheard of – undreamt. That grace will come I am sure – from whom I don't pretend to guess. Spiritual grace is a fact

– we see it in a greater or lesser degree in all the chosen, and it comes from some power not governed by terrestrial forces. It is a love that surpasses all understanding – that asks nothing but to be a sacrifice on the great Altar of Love. You don't have to know the God that gave this gift to us, only to know that it is existent, unquenchable, and inexhaustible, is sufficient religion for all. Its infusion is a matter of time. Our faith is our own. Love is the divine gift. There is nothing human in its origin. Love is giving. Love never calculates or asks reward – Love is its own reward. When Love feels cheated, it is not Love; It's the human substitute.

This is an endeavor to make it clear that I think it of little importance that we profess any faith except that of humanity and I hope I have succeeded in relieving your self-reproach. The future will care for itself.

The "Kasdiah" is a book that is necessary because it is the best of Arabic philosophy, and it helps us more impatient ones to be reconciled to slow change. Slow! But inevitable.

15

Uncured Speech

I always liked Billy Strong. Both born in Molowta – we chummed together at school and were pals until he drifted from Colorado to go to the coast.

Billy's father was the minister of our only church and was popular with the best element of the residents. He was never over-censorious of our somewhat ordinary faults and almost tireless when it came to providing recreation for his congregation. Billy's uneventful life had few vicissitudes as a boy, his parents being of moderate means and an assured income.

Graduating from High the same term, we started careers in the home town. I joined my Father in his general store and Billy went to work for Walden who owned the town's one hardware firm.

As in all small towns, there was demand for young men on Sunday and odd nights in the week, Billy and I always met at local entertainments. For so close a friendship we were remarkably dissimilar. I was of small build and slow of speech, while Billy, large, quick-witted and jovial was naturally more popular with both sexes of the younger crowd. No party was complete without Billy Strong and the boy who possessed his friendship had to share his pride with the last girl who had won him as an escort. Always was he at the service of friends and none could wish for more appreciation than we gave him.

When Billy had been with the Walden firm less than six months, he, without due consideration, thought to start a business of his own. He had become familiar with the stock sheets and invoices of Walden's business so naturally he assumed that hardware was the best to get into. Of course, he was against the primary deterrent of most young people wishing to become suddenly independent; he was without capital. In an effort to remedy this deficiency he carried an argument to his friends who unfortunately were as incapable of commanding the missing link as Billy himself. The prospect of his airy business flew in smoke, but the argument, which was a solid one, remained a fact. Everybody had now learnt of Walden's affairs, and it was not long before that firm discovered that prospective customers could ascertain, through Billy, the price of goods they intended to purchase. There was but one outcome. It was either Walden or Billy -- Billy lost.

At the family home, Billy's stigma as a failure was not welcome. His father reproached him with a lack of trustworthiness, and said that for a son of his to be unworthy of responsibility was a reflection upon himself and his profession. Billy, all humility, explained that he had intended no wrong, and accepted his father's argument that business must be confidential, and that an employee cannot become indifferent to his employer's interests.

Billy was eventually taken on as clerk in the lumberyard, and was fortified with sufficient worldly wisdom to assure him a chance of making good. The new job entailed more labor than Billy cared for or had been used to, but this in no way interfered with social activities. His discharge by Walden had not affected his popularity among the younger crowd.

I wish I could say that Billy worked to a position of responsibility; I can't. The manager of the lumber yard slowly found that the town folk were better informed on the price they expected to pay for lumber than upon the price that gave him his profit.

Billy, due to an unquenchable desire to be friendly and impart information, was again unemployed.

At the age of nineteen Billy was "on the street." In the small commercial world of Malowta, he was a "dead one." To stay in the community, he would of necessity have to devote his energies to other than the business life. His father was not a man to refuse a shelter under the paternal roof – and there were his mother's feelings to be considered – but there was little chance for doubt that it was not to be considered permanent. Being reluctant to leave the neighborhood and Ada Milton, his sweetheart, he again looked for a job. Finally he succeeded at Targ Anderson's Dairy, moving to the ranch some ten miles from Malowta.

Here the conditions under which he worked were different to anything he had before experienced. The hours were long and monotonous. He missed the companionship of his friends. Without the stimulation of being appreciated he became less amiable. He got into town to visit for a few hours on Sundays, and the rest of the time it seemed to him he was either milking cows, shoveling or wheeling dung, or going dejectedly to his room to spend long hours in solitude.

The only break in this dullness was the friendly chatter of Mrs. Anderson as she served him his meals. He discovered that upon one point they were in accord – the dairy was a means toward living but not happiness, and their mutual resentment soon induced a sense of fellowship.

Through this state of mind, they drifted into an understanding which Billy disclosed on his visits to town. Whenever I made a trip to the ranch I noticed that he now wore a different air. He swaggered offensively and scorned my judgements. With Ada he still kept company and he called at my rooms nearly every trip, but it was nearer his mood to be with the crowd in the back room of Harley's Pool Parlor, where he was stimulated into talking much, and unwisely.

Close to ten months after taking his job, he arrived late in the night at Malowta and awoke me to listen to a tale of an intimacy, which he called love, (though it appeared to be founded on nothing deeper than propinquity) and of a growing recklessness which had resulted in a frightened woman threatening suicide if he did not provide a home beyond the wrath of a vengeful husband. He plainly showed and expressed fear. Borrowing $50.00 cash and a valise with a few necessities he prepared to leave town. Shortly before daylight without making further visits, he boarded the train that passed through Malowta bound for the coast.

Targ Anderson was in town in the morning. He hung around the streets without making a confident of anyone. Due to Billy's talkativeness, he had no information which would be news to the town.

The opinions of the gossips ranged from the extreme of regret that Billy had made a get-away and beaten Malowta out of the thrill of an up-to-date tragedy, to those who held Billy in enough regard to feel relieved that he had escaped the penalty of his bad faith.

Anderson returned to his ranch that night, bringing his wife back with a trunk and bag in the morning. She took a West bound train. Anderson, after spending an hour with an attorney, went to his ranch without satisfying the town's curiosity.

It was five years before Malowta again heard of Billy Strong, then I received a letter from San Francisco. It was written on stationery which notified the receiver that Wm. Strong was the General Manager of the Kismet Importing and Trading Company, and that an Abner Kleim was the Selling Agent. The firm's office was on Market Street, with a further notice that immediate attention was given to all orders.

A page of this letter was filled with declarations that California had proven to be the promised land. In it was the several times repeated assertion, boastingly expressed, that he was doing well. There were digs at the sleepiness of the home burg and its stay-at-homes.

He enclosed two $100.00 postal orders and one for $70.00 (though why the Kismet Company banked through the Post Office, I did not understand) and I was commissioned to give the $200.00 to his mother. The $70.00 was to reimburse me for the valise and money I had loaned him on his leaving Malowta.

He said that being now started toward success he could, with better grace, renew his intimacy with his folks. He closed with a request for some news of the town, and the information that he was married.

I wrote in reply and congratulated him on his success. I told him of the births and the deaths, and that Ada Milton had married the owner of the town garage, and also, that on account of my father's death, I had inherited the store and the home.

In the next year I wrote him two or three times in response to letters from him. I learned that he also corresponded with his mother and contributed comfortable sums toward her welfare.

As I was now sufficiently established to support a family, I had decided to marry. Partly from curiosity and partly from a desire for a long-deferred vacation, my fiancé and I decided to spend our honeymoon in California, and so wrote Billy who replied with a cordial invitation to look him up when we came to San Francisco.

Spending a month in the southern part of the state, we arrived in San Francisco, and after settling in a quiet hotel, I called up Billy at the address of the Kismet Company. He was out, so I left a message informing him of our hotel.

The next morning at eleven, the elevator boy brought up the card of Mr. Strong, representing the Kismet Importing and Trading Company. I went down to the lobby and eagerly looked over the faces to find that of my old friend. I would not have been sure that the large, well-dressed stranger were he, if I had not seen his face light up with recognition when he saw me. We shook hands warmly, but as I watched him I was somehow conscious of a feeling of disappointment; there was certainly nothing definable; he was expensively dressed, full of assurance – yet the sense of disappointment lingered. I asked him to lunch and he countered with an invitation for my wife and I to go out to lunch with him. My wife joining us at this time, she and Billy, who had been friends from childhood at home, renewed their acquaintanceship. Billy accepted our invitation to lunch conditionally that we should dine with he and his wife that night.

At seven o'clock the Strong's called for us at our hotel. After mutual introductions, with a slight embarrassment on Billy's part, it occurred to me that Mrs. Strong was the late Mrs. Anderson. My wife although unacquainted with Mrs. Anderson, sensed my knowledge and shot an interrogative glance in my direction which I confirmed. Neither one of us felt obligated to assume the role of moral censor, or to interject an unpleasantness that might spoil the evening.

We went to a palace of entertainment, where to our conceptions the splendor was all out of proportion to the ordinary individual's income. Billy ordered lavishly and the ease with which the wine appeared on the table rather astonished us who were strange to the life.

Warming in the glow of a very good wine, Billy talked wildly. He poked fun at my business and myself, pointing out that I could stay in Malowta a thousand years and never see anything or get anywhere. He bragged on the money he had and what he expected to have; told us of a $12,000.00 home which he was building down the Peninsular. He went into details of the fittings and furnishings which were obviously being done in a costly manner. He insisted that we should accompany him down to view the "bungalow" in the morning, an invitation which we accepted.

Alice and I began to feel that the pace was getting a little too swift for our standards, although nothing really offensive had occurred. After all, when a large, generous and prosperous individual whom you have known all your life, starts to grand-eloquently declaim his own importance, you can hardly construe it into a slight, but to us the quiet of the hotel would have been preferable.

The hours passed, and the dishes were cleared away. It seemed quite unexpected that anyone should relinquish their table. The dark colored glasses contained the wine; the bottles, thinly disguised, were standing on the floor; voices became louder; restraint slipped away and between the numbers of the vaudeville program the dance floor was covered with frolicsome diners. To us it was a scene of wonderment and surprise, and curiosity held us more strongly than any other impulse. Well we knew that we would not likely see such a scene again.

As the night progressed, it was certain that Billy's acquaintanceship was wide and varied. We met his associate, Mr. Kleim, who appeared to be more of a business man than Billy. They both spoke familiarly and often confidentially to many men, whose common characteristic seemed to be that they were all expensively dressed. I would have placed them in a category ranging from the top to the bottom of society.

At one o'clock, Alice and I, feeling satiated with gaiety, broke away, although we were assured that the night was only just beginning. Certain that we had seen all of it that we wished to, we made a date with Billy for ten o'clock in the morning and taxied home to the hotel and to bed.

In the morning at ten o'clock, my wife and I sat in the lobby awaiting Billy's arrival when a boy paged me for a phone call. Billy was on the phone. He wished, with apologies, to call off until sometime in the following week, the trip to his new home. He said he had an important business engagement for that afternoon which necessitated him leaving town. He asked if I would excuse him to my wife and come down and take lunch with him alone before he departed.

My wife wishing to take in the Art Palace – a subject in which I was little interested – I accepted Billy's invitation. Having secured the address of the place to meet him, I explained to my wife, and left for the appointment on foot.

I found Billy in a soft drink and cigar parlor on Kearny Street. The place was comparatively crowded with fully fifteen men standing around in groups. My mind recorded that they were not of the character that I would personally choose as companions, but as we were in the shadow of the Hall of Justice and Billy seemed familiar with them, I thought there could be little unpleasantness to a stranger.

Billy was much excited and had undoubtedly taken several drinks of strong water. He asked me to drink and I took a lemonade. Billy took something else. He was nervous.

During the lunch which we took in a neighboring chop house, he told me that he was on the border of a big deal, and if he pulled it, would be on easy street. Evidently it was something of considerable importance to him as he was unable to talk of anything else.

He asked me to be sure and remain in San Francisco until his return as he wished his mother to have a first-hand description of his prospective home.

As we sat in the semi-curtained cubby in which the meal had been served, a man who had evidently just eaten stood in the entrance and saluted Billy with, "Hello Boy. How's things?"

I recognized one of the loungers from the soft drink parlor and again mentally questioned Billy's choice of friends.

With an effort to appear off-hand, Billy said, "Oh, so, so."

The stranger dropped his voice and said, "Well, you did pretty well with the Dinah."

Billy, with a quick glance around, replied shorty, "Not so bad."

"Well, she's gone back to Vancouver, hasn't she?"

Billy, -- with an assumed indifference --, "Maybe."

"I guess you killed Bonita Beach so that you guys'll never pull anything there again," said the stranger.

"Oh, I don't know."

"You guys are pikers," continued the man tauntingly, "A coupl' cases and you think you've got somethin'. A couple of trucks would be nearer to my size. Well, you'll never pull it twice on that landing."

"Oh, I don't know that they're so wise."

"It ain't that they're so clever, it's that you ain't got the guts."

Billy, with rising heat, "Well, I'm going to show them something before the moon is much older."

"Not at the same landing."

"I don't see why. I found it first."

"Well, luck to you, if you can make it."

"You watch me if you don't think I can put it over."

"Oh, I didn't say you couldn't Billy. So-long." And he strolled out.

Billy turned to me and said irritably, "Now you know, Max. I'm running IT. And I don't give a damn who knows it. You, Max, were born to be a plodder. I've always wanted to take a chance on something that wasn't easy. I guess I shouldn't have shot off my head, but these snoopers make me sick. They think I haven't the nerve, but I'm going to show them before tomorrow that I have. I'm going to clean up $40,000.00 tonight and then quit. I'll show those geeks in Malowta that I'm no piker. You think I'm wrong, but I know I'm right. They kicked me half a dozen times before I took a tumble. This game was my chance and I took it. I'll be on easy street and then you can all say what you damn please.

This revelation considerably distressed me. I can't say I was shocked, because I knew such adventures were undertaken. I also knew that I was sorry that I had come in contact with it, but I felt no necessity to protest in any way.

Billy and I went out of the restaurant and walked half a block toward Market Street. Coming alongside of a large limousine with the curtains drawn, Billy said, "This is my car. Now we say good-by. Wish me luck."

Then, I – strict for all forms of law – wished him luck. Glancing in the back of the limousine, I caught a glimpse of three hard faces – and mentally I again wished him luck.

After the big car swung down the street, I felt relieved that I was alone, and turned to the hotel.

In my room, I pondered over the events of the day. So this was this was the source of Billy's prosperity. My mind went back to Malowta. I pictured the various "I told you so's." I could sense the pain of Mr. and Mrs. Strong if their son should hold them up to local scorn, and their humiliation for the pride they had taken in the remittances they had received through the grace of this illicit trade.

Alice did not return from the Art Palace until supper time. I told her everything that had occurred. There was a teasing light in her eye when she asked, "Why didn't you go along?"

I countered with, "I already have an established business and don't wish to get into another."

She said, "Yes, but you might have gotten a kick out of this one."

Which I thought was rather an unfair comparison of Bill's irregular life and my own, but I believe the best of women have an unexplainable sympathy for the Ishmaelites among us.

The next day Billy occupied much of our thoughts. We wondered if he would call-up before night.

Returning from the Museum in the Park, we saw in an evening paper the headline, "MAN KILLED AT BONITA BEACH." As I had never heard of Bonita Beach before yesterday, I was struck with the coincidence, but in no way sensed a tragedy.

We bought a paper and saw that a well-dressed and unidentified man had been found murdered close to the landing pier. Nothing suggested that this stranger was Billy. Neither did we think it was Billy, but because he had gone to Bonita Beach in a surreptitious manner, we felt intimately associated with this tragedy.

When we came from supper, the papers supplied further details. They stated that the unknown dead was suspected of being the victim of hi-jackers. Now for the first time, it seemed possible that it might be Billy.

While debating whether to go to our room or take in a moving picture, a telephone call came. It was from Mrs. Strong. The dead man was Billy. I hurried out to her apartment on Sutter Street to give what sympathy I was able. I found her much upset, but her anger somewhat balanced her grief. She told me that the first knowledge came from Kleim who had it from one of the truck drivers Billy had hired to bring the liquor to the city. This driver told him that after they had secured their loads, they had been held up by two strangers who had been assisted by the men Billy had used for unloading the launch. Billy was the only one who attempted a resistance, for which he had been brutally beaten by the men whom he thought were his friends. Substitute drivers, already provided, had been put on the trucks. The hi-jackers, either to leave no clue, or to return to the city had also taken Billy's car.

The truck drivers (as anxious to avoid the prohibition men as the hi-jackers) had walked along the beach to the Cliff House where, securing a car they had brought news of Billy's fate to Kleim.

Mrs. Strong often broke her story of these details to speculate where the three trucks of booze were, and the possibilities of their recovery. In this direction I positively refused to give any assistance. I also decided not to see Billy's body, which was now at an undertaker's. I learnt the inquest was set for eleven o'clock in the morning.

When I returned to the Hotel and told Alice, she was greatly upset. My intimacy with the details, and her unquestioned affection for Billy made this episode in our honeymoon a very grievous shock.

The inquest proved little. There were no witnesses, and except the body of the murdered man, no evidence. The jury was able to establish his identity; proved that he had been robbed as well as murdered; suggested that he was killed while unloading liquor, and brought in a verdict of murder against a party or parties unknown. I was not at the inquest but accepted from the widow, an invitation to the funeral at Cypress Lawn the following day.

That afternoon, feeling restless, depressed, and a little dazed at the events so rapidly occurring, I wandered down Kearny Street to see if something would suggest to me a course of action in a position wherein I had no intimation of the wisest procedure.

I walked the block several times on the opposite side of the cigar parlor where I had met Billy by appointment only forty-eight hours before. Once I stepped in and bought cigars. The crowd looked much the same as they did on my last visit, but whether they were the same or entirely different men, I could not tell.

Half a block down, I saw standing at another cigar counter the tall fellow who had spoken to Billy when I was with him in the restaurant. Stepping to the counter I again bought undesired cigars. Whether this man recognized me or not, I did not know. He certainly showed no fear of a recognition.

Coming down on the other side of the street a few minutes later, I saw him still standing in the same place. I casually asked a policeman (who was apparently off duty and holding up an electric light pole) if he knew who the party across the street was. The policeman giving a casual glance, dropped his eyes and said, "Do you mean the big guy standing on the right-hand side?"

I said, "Yes."

"That's Ed Forney. He did a stretch of seven at San Quentin. He's paroled since last May."

"Well," I asked, "What does he do now?"

"Search me. We've got nothing on him. Don't hear of him working any. I've heard tell he's done some hi-jacking, but nobody I know is hep if he's pulled anything. You can't tell a damn thing about what side of the fence a fellow's on in the booze game. I don't think Ed'll tackle anything unless he's covered. I know he's got friends who would make hell of a squeal if a cop got gay. It ain't a very wise guy that bucks himself out of a job, and I ain't looking to hold up a slab of granite on my chest either."

I thanked the policeman and started to walk on, when emboldened by the confirmation of my bad opinion of the fellow, I decided to again enter the cigar store.

I had heard that often a person under the influence of fear was liable to betray his true state of mind. Selecting a place close to my man's elbow, I asked for a packet of cigarettes. As the clerk turned to get my order a voice said in my ear, "Say, young fellow, have you got anything on your mind?"

I was so astonished I could only reply with a somewhat prolonged "No-o-o."

Forney still looking at me, his eyes expressionless and his mouth only moving said, "Then you'll be better off, stranger, because it's unhealthy to know too much."

Gathering some assurance, I replied, "I can attend to my own business without your advice."

And Forney continuing in the same passionless voice replied, "Of course, you can, young fellow, but seeing you weren't acquainted around here, I felt bit friendly."

When he had started to speak the words came from the center of his mouth but the sentence slowly rippled across his face until it ended in the corner. There was nothing but a quarrel if I continued the conversation and I stepped out and returned to the hotel.

That night I searched for some light to guide my future actions. I had not a shadow of proof to justify making any accusations, and as my assertions would not be evidence I decided I would make none.

The whole booze game seemed to be an evil circle which was as likely to kill itself as to be killed from the outside.

At eight o'clock the following night Alice and I were passengers on the East Bound mail returning to Malowta. In consideration of Mrs. Strong, we had attended the funeral and seen the last of a friend. Returning home we determined to forget the more painful side of the experience.

When I think how far Billy with his gifts might have gone in Maltowa if he had controlled his tongue I feel his death a loss, and the verdict passed on him (in preference to one more sinister and condemnatory) should read:

"He carried the curse of an unstaunched speech."

-ooo-

(a piece of fiction no doubt based on some similar experience)

16

The Ghost of a Love

(Typed from handwritten notes, unfinished)

Of all the strange tales of life and love the World War produced, the strangest was the one about MeeMee and her man Al Horton. The whole world had gone smash.

Life was weird and unreal in those hectic war days. To the boys on leave "wine, women and song" was all that remained. And those who knew could not help but understand—and understanding— would condemn those men who had traveled a thousand miles to hell and back for snatching at the slender thing called "Life" --- desperately hoping to grasp, if only for a moment, eternity—and love.

And so, the boys on leave just naturally gravitated towards MeeMee's Café on Rue....12 in the City of Brest. It was one of the best in town. The men from the American destroyer "Murry" always made the Café their headquarters and the men from "Regament".

It became obvious to all the patrons that the one man in all that .... Gather—ceaselessly coming and going—and a great many men never returning, that the man of MeeMee's choice to the exclusion of all others was Al Horton, chief Radio Operator of the Destroyer "Murry". There were many comments among the boys, complimentary to Mee-Mee and uncomplimentary to her--- and not a little envy. MeeMee was a beautiful French girl who knew much of death and suffering. The war had already taken her Father, her brothers, her uncle, and she had also lost her Mother since the beginning of the war. MeeMee had inherited the Café from her Father and had determined to make a success of it and was doing nicely.

The boys on leave were in a habit of running out of funds and to a few favorites MeeMee extended credit, but experience had taught her the folly of this, so gradually only a very few were trusted.

Al Horton never worried about funds. MeeMee's purse and heart were his. Al helped serve the drinks when in port and he was the only one permitted in her private living quarters...exquisitely and elaborately furnished. It was customary for dinner and drinks to be served in MeeMee's quarters whenever Al was on leave.

MeeMee accepted him and Al accepted what she gave—she was Al's girl. Then there was that week's leave which MeeMee and Al spent together in Paris. She knew Paris and they made all the points of interest. This was war and men were losing love forever. How little it all matters.

Back in Brest after their week's furlough, Al was more and more the envy of his shipmates. Any one of them would have given their chances in heaven to have MeeMee rushing down the street—attired in her finest --- to greet them as they came off duty, but she had only eyes for Al—and no doubt Al swaggered at his luck in capturing the fairest in the town of Brest.

Not one of all those hundreds who envied his good fortune ever suspected the truth and Al was very careful to play the role right to the end. They would not believe the truth if it were told—MeeMee gave him tenderness, funds, drinks on tick and devotion, even shared her bed but not herself. When Al pressed her for a reason—arguing passionately that this was war and other girls were generous enough. She only shook her head and said rather sadly, "That is alright if they want to; it is not wrong, only wrong for me. MeeMee's code was one of her own making. Her morals strangely idealist in a mad world where "men were losing love forever."

17

The Story of Capt. Alan R. I. Hiley coming to Felton

Glengarry Road
Felton, California

Alan R. I. Hiley was living in Los Angeles at the time of the 1906 Earthquake and fire in San Francisco. He was in love with a girl name Nora May French, a poetess, then living in San Francisco. When the news of the disaster broke he tried to get word through to San Francisco but it was impossible. He decided to come up

Capt. Alan R. Hiley arriving amidst Redwoods
ARH archive, editor

from the South and check himself. When he finally found Nora May French, she was camping in the park with many thousands of others, happy and delighted with the adventure. On his return, when he arrived in San Jose he recalled that a second-hand book dealer in Los Angeles named Nathan L. Greist had moved to Santa Cruz. Alan Hiley decided to take the train from Los Gatos and call on this man. He found him in the second-hand book business in Santa Cruz. Nothing would do but they must make the trip to the Greist cabin in the Redwoods and stay overnight. Mr. Greist hitched up the buggy and the horse and they made the trip up the road then known as the Big Tree Road.

That night in the Redwoods, that trip up the San Lorenzo Drive, the quiet and the peace was too much for the adventurous Alan Hiley. He completely succumbed to the spell of the Redwoods. He returned to Los Angeles, sold out all his holdings, shipped his personal effects to Santa Cruz and followed. For six months he studied the area, the maps, the history of the country. Not only the Big Trees area but Bonny Doon, Soquel, etc. However, it is fairly evident that the San Lorenzo country intrigued him. He heard that the Hihn Co. had 32 acres for sale fronting on the present San Lorenzo Drive, officially known as Highway 9. He bought the 32 acres. There was a small cabin—the same house now rebuilt and owned by the Ben Sherman family, then the DeWald Place.

He cleared the land and put thousands of dollars of stove wood into Santa Cruz. The only catch was that whenever he delivered a load of wood and the buyer failed to pay, the profit and many loads of wood disappeared. He was running too close for such pitfalls.

When the land was cleared of brush and only the larger trees remained he went into partnership with a man and laid out 46 lots known as the Big Trees Park Subdivision. (Map) Here you will see for the first time the name of GLENGARRY ROAD. At the time the subdivision was mapped the County of Santa Cruz accepted the Glengarry Road as a County Road. But it took almost 30 years before they did any upkeep on it. When the Subdivision was ready to be put on the market Alan Hiley asked his partner what the buyers were going to do for water. He said they could go plumb to ---- for water or words to that effect. Alan Hiley saw red. He started to buy the partner out and the partner decided he wouldn't sell. So a suit was started. Alan Hiley won; the partnership was dissolved and the water system installed.

by Alma Hiley Cain, 25 October, 1956

18

Letter Excerpts & Notes

Excerpt copy of letter:
21 January 1923
Dear Dolly: (his sister D. Frances P. Hiley)
I can't imagine myself at any stage of my life on a winning side. I always purposely pick the losers. I know when I went to Texas, soon after, Yankee was a term of insult, yet I was, for contrariness a champion of the negro and somewhat got myself disliked as a "negro lover".

Here in California today where we have a "Jap Question", I am defending the Japanese to the indignation of many.

Mother, I think was always my inspiration. I tried to carry through her upright and direct code. In my formative years on the Brazilian Coast, years with a coat, seldom shoes, nothing but a single shirt and a pair of pants.

I wore her gold ring inscribed with "Heilig" *("Holy")* in blue enamel. One day on a German brig, while sliding down a wire backstay a loose wire ran between the ring and my finger, broke the ring and nearly took the finger off. I had no place to hide it. My possessions beside the clothes I wore was a half blanket and no mattress, so I hid it under the bunk. Of course it was stolen-- and I was later thrown unconscious into a hospital and the ship sailed with my pay.

Several times in my life during a prosperous era and a flow of sentiment I have considered having a duplicate made which would be ridiculous because no gold ring would stand the hard usage and it looks too much like display to occasionally wear a ring.

Anyway, if I believed in a future life the judge who I would most wish to commend me would be Mother.

I also have a strong affection for Grandmother's old nose wrinkling into a sniff when she thought she scented something sneaky.

Charley I imagine is a good man who has everyone's respect, but most of the goodness in this world is lack of individualism. It takes sinners to make saints and most sinners have struggled harder to qualify to respect than those that were just born that way and "growed up".

(Written on page but apparently not included in letter):

I love Mother; not because she was my mother but because she was a Mother.

-

Letter excerpt probably to Frances, possibly Sybil:
30th December 1926

In Father's youth, 1860. To break the herd law was heresy. The voice of the independent thinkers was almost inarticulate. The disciples few; Only the most ardent could decipher the signs at the cross-roads.

Then he sprang from at least three generations of ultra-orthodox. His every tradition was to "conform". This I sensed. I could find no guide. All I knew was that it wasn't ME. The best I knew was to become a pilgrim. Because false scents led me in bye-paths was not my fault (or his) ---Only—I would spare my son. Fortunately today the course is better charted.

In reconstructing – Mother's ambition was to raise a male child into something modeled on the standard of what she thought a man should be. Bless Her. If she had been given another ten years she might have succeeded. She had the hands and also the clay.

All this I tried to say to you months since when I sent you the poem:
"I was made of this and this
An angel's prayer and a gypsy's kiss"

I expected you to transpose the sex.

Someday I will send you my memories of Mother's death. It is written: But I am not satisfied with it. It may be a little unfair to myself in its present form. My callousness at the actual ceremony, irritation at the forms etc., are too lurid, and my sense of loss only came when I was back on the *Worcester*.

An English person has a hypocritical pose of pretending its bad form to talk of themselves. Doubtless it is in minor matters but I know that it is the most interesting subject that any person can discuss and the one that to them is not only the most vital; but the source of the greatest knowledge of themselves and thus of others. It is only by analyzing our own reactions that we can arrive at any understanding of those of others. And as we are more intimate with our own environment and hereditary it gives us a base from which to start reasoning from.

Notes from ledger:

(from ARH childhood experiences) Father was amiable and gifted but conservative and intensely orthodox. He understood his children and loved them when they showed they had inherited any of his excellent gifts—if he made any mistake with us it was from not reasoning that it was possible the children might lean more towards the maternal side than his own, and he failed in a sense of humor when unable to recognize and condone these traits when they appeared. I was and am my mother's child and as such could not follow my father in his acceptances of rules by the yardstick and with respect to the fate of those boys who attempted to modernize Elisha.

I think what was most beneficial to me in training was the compulsory table manners. Although at the time it appeared exaggerated and unnecessary, the habit formed of unconsciously considering the comfort of others unfolds into a higher feeling when experience has taught you the laws of suffering.

I think parents often make a mistake. Walter and I were very similar in temperament but he being the eldest, was always reminded he would eventually represent the family, inherit its substance and be responsible for its good name.

If we went swimming or shooting, it was he that should see I didn't drown or shoot myself or somebody else. This always rankled. I did not see why I could not be responsible for myself if not for others. This ignoring my reliability always stung and I showed my resentment by acting the character I was accredited with. And at afterlife it has demonstrated itself in a passion to boss every undertaking I've become interested in whether digging a post hole or running a mine. I could have been more normal with a few grains of faith. A suspicion of myself was incubated that I've never lost.

Temma—The affectionate manner in which she intoned her pet name for me- "Alan-a-dale" was to stay with me for life.

I have had one moving spirit in life—it may seem brag to say so—but it's the motif of nearly every important act of my life—a sympathy with a loser and a hatred of bullies – a sense of Justice which has compelled me into a life of losing fights for the other guy—the fellow whom I happen to think at the time is getting a raw deal. I went into the Boer war without one idea that victory was possible for them—my knowledge of England's power and resources was established but I wished to help, let them know they'd been in a fight when it was over.

19

Reflection

Occasionally a man who is fairly self-sufficient will try to explain himself to someone whom he respects. He really is not so much interested in convincing his audience as himself. He cannot understand some of his own motives and is seeking a key from a sympathetic listener.

I have a complex which is scorn of money; it has been with me always and causes me to do from a worldly point of view the most irrational things. It's the key to my character – life – action. My conduct to others has appeared semi-mad – yet to me was natural. At times I've given largely with apparent generosity. It really was nothing of the kind. If I was not immediately in need of food, shelter, or clothes -- I was only parting with something that had no value to me, something I didn't want. Twenty-five years past – puzzled and knowing I was something abnormal, I sought a solution of how I was to maintain my independence without a change of method, and I decided that solution was the elimination of luxuries.

I was not unsuccessful in a business sense. As a mining man, I produced dividends, but these only interested me in as far as they could be used for further development. I wanted to do it again somewhere that the ground was untried.

Alan R. Hiley
ARH archive, editor

At sixty, I think I have discovered the key. I was born to wealth and at twelve the contrast between our own living conditions and those of our employees filled me with doubt. Seeking a solution of the apparent injustice, I was given none. It had just happened. This didn't satisfy me. I left, seeking conditions more compatible to my sense of the fitness of things. I've never found them but the childhood lesson made a permanent impression. Since then at various times several fortunes have been laid in my lap. I could reach out at will and pull one in when desired. I've never been interested. Giving or refusing the stuff meant nothing to me. I see where I have lacked prudence but have no regrets. With an unprotected old age, I know I've been compensated for what monetary loss I have foregone. If I had done otherwise I would have lost all I most value in my character and life. Because mine is a real scorn of money and its inherent injustice and not to be mistaken for the pretended scorn so many assume to disguise their envy – hatred or malice. Provided you are sensitized the stuff is not worth the bitterness involved in its possession --- anyway in quantities. Hence if my peculiarity happens to have brought some difficulties, it is also (up to date) responsible for my happiness.

A. R. H.
25th November 1929

*You are the deep innerness of all things,
the last word that can never be spoken.
To each of us you reveal yourself differently:
to the ship as coastline, to the shore as a ship.*

~ Rilke

Notes on the Family

An affectionate description of *Rev. Walter Hiley* and the school at Hyde Hall can be found in Albert Baillie's autobiography. *Henrietta Jemima Forbes Hiley* helped manage, run and fund the schools headed by Walter. *Alan* and *Charlie* were the two sons who settled in the United States after other adventures. *Charles* initially settled in Florida, worked for a time as a guard in Western Australia, and farmed in Florida, Colorado and Alabama. Of a strong philosophic bent, he was also a painter. After his wife's sudden death, he returned to the countryside outside of Orlando, worked and painted until heart problems caused him to move to his daughter Margaret's in Minnesota. *Walter* Jr. died suddenly of an infection at 22 years of age. *Daisy* (Margaret) lived for only 1 ½ years, taken by a bout of meningitis and whooping cough. *Ranald* settled in Australia. *Ernest* remained in England, though he managed railway projects in India, Mexico, South Africa, New Zealand and England, later becoming Sir "Haviland" Hiley. *Sibyl* spent time in New Zealand and Australia, visited the US brothers, but remained in England. *Frances*, the youngest, was among the trailblazing women newly graduated from Somerville College, Oxford University. She distinguished herself as Headmistress of Newcastle Girls Upper School, where a building bears her name, and which operates today. She served for a time as president of the Philosophical and Literary Society in Newcastle-upon-Thames, and was a published author. And there is the unsung *Alma Graun Hiley Cain* who courageously took on the adventure of life on the hilltop, with its hardships and beauty, knowing she would be raising her son alone, and who faithfully preserved Alan's legacy.

Additional Photos

Henrietta Jemima Forbes, 1872,

Henrietta and child

Henrietta & Walter Hiley

Grandparents Graun, Charles Forbes Hiley, chaplain, Alma Hiley, Alan R., Jr.

Other Publications

Other Published works by Alan R.I. Hiley

The Mobile Boer: Being the Record of the Observations of Two Burgher Officers. co-authored with John Arthur Hassell. New York: Grafton Press, 1902.

Articles in the *LA Times*:

"Enemies of the Rattler: Modes of Attack Practiced by Roadrunners and Eagles," June 4, 1904.

"Casa Grande. The Oldest Building in the Southwest," July 31, 1904.

"An Unseen Foe. A Story of the Black Hills of Dakota," Sept, 1904 (name misspelled as Haley)

"The Last 'Long Tom': The Tragedy of a Soldier's True Love," July 3, 1904.

Publications authored by D.F.P. Hiley

Dorothea Frances Poles Hiley *(known as Frances, and Aunt Dolly by family)* published under the name D.F.P. Hiley.

Ports & Happy Havens. Newcastle: Patrick & Page, 1924.

Italian Negatives. Newcastle: Patrick & Page, 1921.

Pedagogue Pie. London: Ivor Nicholson, 1936.

Unspoken Speeches to Parents. Newcastle: Patrick & Page, 1923.

"The Soil, the Seed, and the Sower," in *The Headmistress Speaks*, London: Kegan Paul, Trench, Trubner & Co., 1937, p. 127.

References

"I Follow a Tutor and the Hunt," *My First Eighty Years*. Albert Victor Baillie. London: John Murray, 1951.

Rilke's Book of Hours. Trans. by Anita Barrows and Johanna Macy. New York: Riverhead Books, 1996.

Nature Meditations. Hazrat Inayat Khan. New Lebanon, NY: Omega Publications, 2005.

The Sufi Message, Vol. V. Hazrat Inayat Khan. Geneva: Barrie and Rockliff, 1962.

Sholem imprint on page vii is from letterhead made for Alan's stationery.

Acknowledgments

My thanks to, and in memory of, Alan and Betty Hiley, Alma Graun Hiley Cain, D.F.P. Hiley, and Peter Hiley for the many stories, and to my own father Alan Ernest MacDonald Hiley. Appreciation to Robert Stewart.

Thanks to Peter Clark and Wendy Waite in England for help in Sawbridgeworth and Brent Pelham; to Ted Barclay for information about the house & history in Brent Pelham; to Hector Rogers and Stroma at the Glengarry Heritage Centre in Invergarry, Scotland, to Jeanetta McCallum of Invergarry; to W. & C. Hiley for welcoming me.

And a special thanks to Naomi Rose a gifted book midwife who generously encouraged me.

Alan R. I. Hiley, 1896
ARH archive, editor

Capt. Alan Richard Illeigh Hiley was a philosophical adventurer and author, who after a far-flung life of adventure and misadventure, settled at last on a peaceful hilltop in the Coastal Redwood Range of Santa Cruz County, where he homesteaded, chopped wood and reflected on his life's journey with honesty, insight and humor.

Janet A. Hiley, MS, Editor, occupational therapist and artist, is Faculty Emerita of the Cabrillo College Stroke Center in Santa Cruz County California, a strength-affirming educational community for adults who have experienced life-changing health events.

www.ingramcontent.com/pod-product-compliance
Lightning Source LLC
Chambersburg PA
CBHW031248290426
44109CB00012B/485